The First Horsemen

The Emergence of Man

The First Horsemen

by Frank Trippett
and the Editors
of Time-Life Books

TIME-LIFE BOOKS
New York

TIME-LIFE BOOKS

FOUNDER: Henry R. Luce 1898-1967

Editor-in-Chief: Hedley Donovan
Chairman of the Board: Andrew Heiskell
President: James R. Shepley
Group Vice President: Rhett Austell

Vice Chairman: Roy E. Larsen

MANAGING EDITOR: Jerry Korn
Assistant Managing Editors: Ezra Bowen,
David Maness, Martin Mann, A. B. C. Whipple
Planning Director: Oliver E. Allen
Art Director: Sheldon Cotler
Chief of Research: Beatrice T. Dobie
Director of Photography: Melvin L. Scott
Senior Text Editor: Diana Hirsh
Assistant Art Director: Arnold C. Holeywell

PUBLISHER: Joan D. Manley
General Manager: John D. McSweeney
Business Manager: John Steven Maxwell
Sales Director: Carl G. Jaeger
Promotion Director: Paul R. Stewart
Public Relations Director: Nicholas Benton

THE EMERGENCE OF MAN

SERIES EDITOR: Dale M. Brown
Editorial Staff for *The First Horsemen*:
Text Editors: L. Robert Tschirky, Johanna Zacharias
Picture Editor: Kathy Ann Ritchell
Designer: Albert Sherman
Assistant Designer: Elaine Zeitsoff
Staff Writers: Susan Hillaby, Malabar Hornblower, Jill Spiller
Chief Researcher: Peggy Bushong
Researchers: Josephine Reidy, Robin Richman, Carolyn Stallworth
Design Assistant: Lee W. Nevitt

Editorial Production
Production Editor: Douglas B. Graham
Assistant Production Editor: Gennaro C. Esposito
Quality Director: Robert L. Young
Assistant Quality Director: James J. Cox
Copy Staff: Rosalind Stubenberg (chief), M. Caputineanu-Minden,
Elaine Pearlmutter, Florence Keith
Picture Department: Dolores A. Littles, Marianne Dowell
Traffic: Feliciano Madrid

Valuable assistance was given by the following departments and
individuals of Time Inc.: Editorial Production, Norman Airey; Library,
Benjamin Lightman; Picture Collection, Doris O'Neil; Photographic
Laboratory, George Karas; TIME-LIFE News Service, Murray J. Gart;
Correspondents Felix Rosenthal, John Shaw (Moscow), Elisabeth Kraemer
(Bonn), Dorothy Bacon and Margot Hapgood (London), Ann Natanson
(Rome), Maria Vincenza Aloisi and Josephine du Brusle (Paris), Helga
Kohl (Athens), Traudl Lessing (Vienna), Mehmet Ali Kislali (Ankara) and
Eva Stichova (Prague).

The Author: FRANK TRIPPETT, formerly a senior editor of *Look*
magazine, is a freelance writer. He has published articles on a
wide variety of subjects and has twice shared the National
Headliner Award for distinguished reporting of public affairs.
He is the author of *The States: United They Fell*, an analysis
of state legislatures.

The Consultants: DR. RUTH TRINGHAM is Assistant Professor
of Anthropology at Harvard University, where she lectures
on the prehistoric cultures of eastern Europe and the U.S.S.R.
She received her doctorate at Edinburgh University in 1966,
and has also studied at the universities of Prague and Leningrad. In 1971 she published a book, *Hunters, Fishers and
Farmers of Eastern Europe, 6000-3000 B.C.*, about the origins
of agriculture and metalworking in that area. DR. ALEKSANDR
M. LESKOV, a consultant for the text chapters of this volume,
is a member of the Ukrainian Academy of Sciences. He spe-
cializes in the archeology of the Bronze and Iron Age cultures
of southeastern Europe, particularly those of the Cimmerians,
who were the pre-Scythian inhabitants of the south Russian
steppe, and the Scythians themselves. Over the past 13 years,
he has excavated about 400 burial mounds in the Ukraine.
JOHN K. ANDERSON is Professor of Classical Archeology at the
University of California at Berkeley. He has participated in
several archeological excavations in Turkey and Greece and
has written numerous articles dealing with ancient horsemanship and military tactics, as well as several books on those
subjects, including *Ancient Greek Horsemanship* and *Military
Theory and Practice in the Age of Xenophon*.

The Cover: Hunting on horseback without benefit of stirrups,
a group of Fourth Century B.C. Scythians churn up the summer dust of the south Russian steppe. One rider reaches for
the reins of a runaway horse, while the others gallop with
their bows at the ready. Painting directly on a photograph of
present-day Afghani horsemen, Michael A. Hampshire added
authentic Scythian touches to their dress and regalia. He also
created the illustrations for the essay on the Scythian way of
death that appears on pages 117 through 125.

Contents

Introduction

This is a book about the relationship between human beings and the horse, and the impact of that relationship upon the technology and the horizons of mankind. Unfortunately the archeological record of the revolutionary role of the horse as a mount is scant. And indeed the emergence, sometime during the First Millennium B.C., of the first horse-riding peoples on the steppes of Eurasia has long been veiled in mystery. Until recently there was little proof of their existence other than what their graves yielded. Thus, for archeologists like myself, knowledge of these peoples was limited to their customs in honoring their dead. We knew virtually nothing of how the prehistoric steppe inhabitants lived, how they obtained their food or what their settlements and camps looked like. Yet how could we complete a picture of the first horsemen with such vital pieces missing?

Fortunately Soviet archeologists have been excavating sites where steppe peoples lived—along the Don, Volga and Dnieper rivers, as well as in Central Asia. The findings are no less spectacular than new discoveries of several dazzling tombs in the Ukraine, and they have served to corroborate previously questioned reports left by ancient historians such as Herodotus, and have in turn been reinforced by observations of the 19th and 20th Century mounted nomads recorded by ethnographers. The extrapolations are valid because the steppe dwellers of today face the same problems, make the same choices and mine the same potentials of life in the grasslands as did the riders of old. And, of course, they too have that special relationship with the horse.

The picture of the first horsemen that has thus been pieced together is very different from that held hitherto by many experts. Why the old view persisted over the years is easy to understand. The image of violent, unrelenting, barbaric mounted hordes bursting onto the civilized urban scene remains a vivid page in history; after all, it has been just 500 years since the Mongols ceased to be a decisive power in Asia and eastern Europe. Time and again that image inspired scholars to theorize that otherwise inexplicable catastrophes—cultural upheavals and the destruction of villages, cities, even whole civilizations—were traceable to marauding horsemen who swept out of the Eurasian steppes in search of fresh pasturage and easy riches.

But the new Soviet finds and the reinterpretation of old discoveries suggest that the destruction wrought by the first horsemen was not so massive as had been thought and that the Mongol state—which included at one time almost the whole of Eurasia—was not the norm but a later and very special development. Instead, the first horsemen seem to have had a complex, often peaceable rapport with the peasant and urban populations of their day.

The old view of the horsemen involved another distortion. They were depicted by the Greeks, by the Persians and by the Chinese as inferior in all but warfare. It has become clear, however, from the writings of the Mongols themselves and from studies of modern mounted nomads, that riders of the steppes have always found their way of life superior. The same attitude must have prevailed among the first horsemen in their heyday—and it makes them, in their independence, a fascinating phenomenon.

Ruth Tringham
Harvard University

Chapter One: The Magnificent Marauders

"Wherever man has left his footprint in the long ascent from barbarism to civilization we will find the hoofprint of the horse beside it." So says one authority on the history of the horse. Whether barbarism has been left behind may remain a question, but there can be no doubt about the role of the horse in the odyssey of man. Without the horse, man would be neither what nor where he is.

The stage on which man first mastered the horse, sometime in the shadows of prehistory, is immense: the 3,500-mile sweep of steppes that spreads across two continents, from Hungary to Manchuria. Here, some 3,000 years ago, emerged a new breed of men with enlarged aspirations: the mounted horsemen. Their advent would alter forever not only the direction and velocity of the human drama, but also the very minds and manners of all the other players. For, once man mounted a horse, he loomed eight feet tall and could outrun all his ancient enemies.

What the horsemen of the steppes called themselves—even after they had assembled in aggressive bands and begun to terrorize the ancient world—is uncertain. Since they did not write, they left no record to enlighten modern archeologists puzzling over their remains. The names by which the most famous of the tribes are best remembered were the conventions of outsiders—Greeks and Chinese who, at various times and places, encountered and wrote about them, referring to them as Scythians, Sarma-

A Scythian warrior wielding a spear charges an adversary on this Fourth Century B.C. gold plaque found in the Crimea. In spite of the plaque's minute dimensions—a bare inch and a half by two inches—the Greek artisan who hammered out the low relief managed to include a remarkable amount of information about the rider's dress and the horse's bridle.

tians, Yueh-Chi and Hsiung-nu. And yet, however different their names may be, all the horsemen of the steppes had much in common.

The first of these mounted nomads to attract the attention of historians were the Scythians. They are the horsemen for whom the record is most complete, enriched not only by the colorful accounts of ancient observers, but by the discoveries of archeologists. Thus the Scythians properly begin this book, and they will reappear throughout, especially as they shed light on the development of horse riding and on the other horsemen of the steppes. They were in all respects a passionate people—bearded men with dark, deep-set eyes, weather-cured faces and long, wind-snarled hair. They drank from the skulls of slain enemies and flaunted the scalps of their foes as trophies. In a time when nations had not yet developed skilled cavalrymen and relied almost entirely on foot soldiers and chariots, the Scythians came riding at the gallop, shooting fusillades of singing arrows from their bows. The arrows were armed with deadly three-edged heads, and as these projectiles rained down on their adversaries, the Scythians would plunge forward as though to engage. Then, in the instant before contact, they would wheel about, launch fresh flights of arrows over the rumps of their retreating horses and, shrieking, thunder away to regroup for a new onslaught, leaving the dust-enveloped enemy in disarray.

Such fluid, foxy, devastating maneuvers must have left the Scythians' unmounted foe feeling that they were at the mercy of centaurs. The Scythians' clothing and accouterments, like their tactics, reflected generations of experience with life spent on horseback. They wore trousers in preference to the long robelike garb of settled men, tucking them into, or gathering them over, pliable boots without heels. The tunics or jerkins that they wore beneath their leather or scale armor were loose about the chest but cut narrow in the sleeves for freedom of movement. Each man carried arrows and bow deftly stashed in a single case—a *gorytus*—worn at the left side. And each carried in a sheath tied to the right thigh a long knife or short sword with a straight blade of bronze or iron. Sometimes warriors also armed themselves with javelins and shields of leather scaled with metal plates. On the move the Scythians seemed a part of their animals, seldom dismounting to eat or drink, quenching thirst and hunger as they rode.

Their horses descended from the herds of wild stock that roamed the steppe. They were "useful, strong ponies, with coarse necks and shoulders, very low withers and coarse heads," says J. K. Anderson, an authority on ancient horses. And yet they had a certain beauty, with fine quarters and graceful tails. The Scythians clipped the normally shaggy manes to prevent them from flying up and interfering with their shooting. They rode on rudimentary saddles made of two pads that probably did little more than protect the thighs from abrasion. There were no stirrups; when stirrups finally appeared centuries later, they required a shift from flat to heeled boots.

Where had they come from, these men who seemed to have been born on horseback? The Scythians themselves had a legend that they sprang from the three sons of a certain Targitaus, a person of supernatural birth who dwelled in the Scythians' Black Sea domain. Together the three brothers ruled the land until four golden implements—a plow, a yoke, a battle-ax and a drinking cup—fell from the sky and suddenly began to blaze. Colaxais, the youngest, proved to be the only one of the brothers who could pick up the burning objects, and thus became sole ruler of the Scythian kingdom.

Some scholars speculate that the Scythians came from the Volga basin and reached the south Russian steppe sometime around 1000 B.C., displacing the Cimmerians, whose homeland it had been. By the end of the Sixth Century B.C. the Scythians' mastery of the horse had made them undisputed rulers of a flat and grassy domain that reached westward along the Azov and Black seas, from the Don River to the mouth of the Danube, embracing almost all of what is now the Ukraine, and northward 400 miles to some nebulous boundary where the steppe vanished into an irregular sprawl of dense forests and marshes (*map, pages 12-13*). Through their might they dominated the farmers on the fringes of the steppe and in its river valleys, and ultimately they dominated even the inhabitants of Olbia, Tyras, Theodosia and other Greek trading colonies on the northern rim of the Black Sea. The city dwellers called the enormous tract of country ruled by the nomads Scythia, and the Greeks, by extension, named the horsemen Scythians.

It was also a Greek who left the first full account of them. Around the middle of the Fifth Century B.C. Herodotus, that indefatigable reporter of antiquity, was in the Black Sea city of Olbia, a trading center at the confluence of the Bug and Dnieper rivers, collecting information that would eventually enable him to compile his celebrated history of the Greek and Persian Wars. There he had ample opportunity to gather material on the Scythians, whose traders were well known in the Greek merchant colonies.

Historians owe much of their knowledge of the Scythians to the Fifth Century B.C. Greek writer Herodotus, represented in this marble bust. Described by Cicero as the Father of History, Herodotus gathered a wealth of information about the Scythians while visiting Olbia, a Greek city on the Black Sea. Some of the information he collected was sheer fable, but much of it has been substantiated by archeological research.

The copious observations of Herodotus, while partly a savory scavenger's stew of legend and folklore, also contain a large helping of facts about the Scythians—truths confirmed by later classical writers and by startling modern archeological discoveries, some of them made only since World War II.

Long before Herodotus studied the Scythians in the Fifth Century B.C., they had been a force to be reckoned with. Indeed, they first entered the historical record in the Seventh Century B.C. as Assyria's ally against the Cimmerians, who had lost their homeland to the Scythians and moved south, making a nuisance of themselves among the civilized people already settled in the area. The horsemen obviously got on well with the Assyrians, for their leader, King Bartatua, married an Assyrian princess in 674 B.C.

A quarter of a century later the Scythians again joined forces with the Assyrians, and participated in the destruction of the kingdom of Urartu, in what is now Armenia, and in the conquest of the Medes, whose country lay just south of the Caspian Sea. Flushed with a sense of their new power, the Scythians lorded it over "upper Asia," perhaps the territory of modern Azerbaijan, for 28 years. During their sway there—almost always in the role of marauders or mercenaries—they made a fearsome name for themselves. Apparently they plundered their way through Palestine right to the border of Egypt; the Pharaoh halted their advance by buying them off. Wherever they appeared, says Herodotus, "everything was overthrown by their licentiousness and neglect."

In 612 B.C. the Medes, having regained their strength, besieged Nineveh, Assyria's capital—and this time fighting at their side were their old ene-

THRACE

CARPATHIANS

Danube River

Dniester River

Prut River

SCYTHIANS

● Moscow

● Kiev

Dnieper River

Volga River

URALS

S

▲ Tyras

■ Melgunov

■ Gaimonov

▲ Olbia

Tovsta ■

■ Chertomlyk

Donets River

Don River

Volga River

Neapolis ▲

■ Solokha

SEA OF AZOV

Theodosia ▲

Tanais ■

Tobol River

Ural River

▲ Athens

BLACK SEA

▲▲ Kerch

■ Kul Oba

Elizavetinskaya ■

Ishim River

Seven Brothers ■

Ulski ■

Kelermes ■

■ Kostromskaya

SARMATIANS

Maikop ■

CAUCASUS

URARTU

ARAL SEA

MEDITERRANEAN

SYRIA

ASSYRIA

● Nineveh

Euphrates River

Tigris River

▲ Sakiz

CASPIAN SEA

Syr Darya

PARTHIA

Amu Darya

PAMIRS

Babylon ▲

Susa ▲

MEDIA

RED SEA

PERSIAN GULF

▲ Persepolis

Indus River

ARABIAN SEA

B E R I A

Lena River

Omsk

Irtysh River

Ob River

Yenisei River

Minusinsk

Shibe Tuekta
Bash Adar ■ Pazyryk
Katanda

LAKE BAIKAL

Amur River

Noin Ula

WU-SUN

LAKE
BALKASH

ZUNGARIA

ALTAI

MONGOLIA

KHINGAN

YUEH-CHIH

TIEN SHAN

GOBI DESERT

HSIUNG-NU

Peking

YELLOW
SEA

Yellow River

THE WIDE, WIDE WORLD OF THE HORSEMEN

The first horsemen's grassy world, the undulating steppes (*see key at right*), stretched almost without interruption from the Danube River to a point just short of the Yellow Sea. The Scythians dominated the region north of the Black Sea, while various other mounted nomads —whose tribal names appear on this map of Eurasia as it was in the Fourth Century B.C.—controlled areas to the east. The steppes were bounded on the north by the taiga, or coniferous forest, and laced here and there with deciduous woodlands; to the south lay deserts and mountains. Important geographical regions, major kingdoms and ancient cities, as well as burial sites, are also located on the map. Modern cities have been included for purposes of orientation.

TAIGA

WOODLAND

STEPPE

DESERT

● Modern Cities
▲ Ancient Cities
■ Burial Sites

Miles   0   500

mies, the Scythians. Nineveh fell to the Medes, and Assyria collapsed. But by the turn of the century, the Medes had had a change of heart about their allies and had driven the Scythians out of western Asia. A legend recounted by Herodotus tells that the Median king invited the Scythian chieftains to a feast, got them drunk and killed them. Their power temporarily broken, the Scythians returned to the south Russian steppe. There they grew strong again, and by 514 B.C. were audacious enough to defy Persia's Darius the Great when he tried to subdue them as a prelude to his planned invasion of Greece.

The Scythians had become a force to be reckoned with in the economic sphere as well. By Herodotus' day they were fabulously wealthy. They taxed all trade that passed through their domain on its way to the Greek trading colonies on the Black Sea. The Greek homeland itself depended upon Scythia as a primary source of wheat as well as other commodities —salt, honey, hides, furs and slaves. In exchange, the Greeks supplied Scythia with jewelry, metalwork, art objects, oils and wines.

In addition to reaping enormous revenues from the trade of neighboring peoples, the Scythians maintained a lucrative commerce with distant suppliers of raw metals. From the Caucasus came iron in abundance, as well as immense quantities of copper and gold. From rich lodes in the Ural Mountains and from sources in the Altai ranges of Central Asia flowed tin and still more gold.

Yet, with all their wealth, the Scythians continued to live primarily by, with and for their herds of cattle, sheep and horses. The livestock provided not only their food but also leather and wool for the clothes on their backs and even for their dwellings—tents of felt that resembled the round yurts still used today by Mongolian nomads. They made the felt for their shelters by wetting and pounding together wool and animal hair until the fibers interlocked, and then weatherproofed the material with grease. Felt tents could be set up with equal ease either on the ground when the horsemen encamped, or on great wagons to shelter families on the move.

And within their steppe domain, the Scythians were almost constantly in motion, pursuing the fresh grasses or seeking relief from winter's cruel blasts. In long straggles of ox-drawn carts and tented wagons paced by herds, pointed and flanked by outriders, they traversed the land with the slow swing of the seasons. From early spring to late fall, they swept hundreds of miles across flatness relieved only by shallow, wooded valleys at the shoulders of rivers. With the coming of winter, they fled to the shelter of these same valleys, and there, in encampments perhaps bolstered by earthworks, they endured the frozen months, awaiting spring.

The Scythians seem to have soaked up their temperament from the steppe and its climate. Scythia was, as the Ukraine is now, the prey of challenging weathers—extreme, volatile, whimsical. Winter entombs the steppe; spring rejuvenates it. For a few months—in a good year—the steppe takes on the aspect of a vast garden as the season unfolds like a giddy jubilation across its whole prodigal expanse. The snow-melt ushers up a bright green patina of moss. New grass pops through the moss in March. Soon the small white blossoms of whitlow (*Draba verna*) shatter the boundless green. Lilac and yellow *Gagea* shoot forth. Then in April tulips join the riot of color, along with purple *Bellevalia sarmatica*—a hyacinth-like plant—and the yellow, blue and violet blossoms of *Iris pumila.*

This gay brilliance is obscured before long by a great wavering froth of silver-green feather grasses. By June the steppe billows like an ocean, while a carpet of blue sage spreads in the shadows of the grasses. Then the relentless sun of summer scathes the vegetation yellow, as scorching winds drive shade temperatures to 104°. By July another feather grass, *Stipa capillata,* hardy enough to withstand all but the driest spells, dominates the steppe with stems that lengthen to six feet and droop to two.

Sudden thunder squalls sometimes drop three inches of rain, as out of an upturned bucket—or cannonade the earth with glistening white hail. A drenching year can yield to one of drought and bristling dust. Still, on good nights the stars glare down with fierce clarity, and dawn can be an explosion.

Like the world around them the Scythians were volatile and exuberant. They could be dark and turbulent or, when times were peaceful and good, bright and breezy. They loved the chase. They enjoyed dancing and singing to the music of drums and stringed instruments resembling lutes, especially during their long winter confinements. The men were famous as hard drinkers of the wines supplied by Greek traders, disdaining the delicate Greek practice of diluting them. On social as well as on ceremonial occasions they used hemp as a narcotic. Herodotus describes them ducking into small, tepee-like felt tents to sniff the vapor arising from hemp seeds in a dish of red-hot stones. "Immediately it smokes," he wrote "and the Scyths, delighted, shout for joy."

Herodotus mistakenly thought that the Scythians also used the vapor-filled tents for sweat baths since they would "never by any chance wash their bodies with water." How the men cleaned themselves no one knows. The women at least did have a cleansing agent, a paste of pounded cypress, cedar and frankincense that, as Herodotus thought, they applied to the face and body: "A sweet odor is thereby imparted to them, and when they take off the plaster on the day following, their skin is clean and glossy."

Herodotus had little to say about the Scythians' manner of dress, but from textile fragments and painted woodwork found in their graves it is plain that they loved bright reds, blues, greens and yellows —colors they no doubt used lavishly in their clothing. The richest graves also produced small gold plaques and strips that had been attached to the garments of both men and women (*pages 24 and 25*). Indulging their passion for ornamentation, the Scythians wore gold torques, diadems, pendants, necklaces, armlets, bracelets, finger rings and earrings—two for a woman, one for a man. The wealthy commissioned or bought jewelry from Scythian or Greek artisans. Many Scythian pieces portrayed animals—stags, horses, felines and fantastic beasts.

The Scythians embellished their horses as opulently as themselves. From their graves have come tinted ivory engravings depicting horses with what looks like saddlery of leather and felt in brilliant colors. Again from the evidence of the graves, the horses of important men wore bridles whose cheekpieces and frontlets flashed with bronze, silver and gold.

Their felt tents, too, must have been awash with decoration and color. The remains of rugs and other fabrics that have been disinterred from tombs give evidence that the interiors were floored with richly patterned carpets, the walls brightened with tapes-

Kirghiz tribesmen of northeastern
Afghanistan, like the steppe nomads of
antiquity, settle down in a winter camp
of felt tents, or yurts, and stone huts.
As evening approaches, the sheep and
goats, let out to pasture during the day,
are corralled to protect them from
wolves and the penetrating night cold.

tries or felt hangings with elaborate appliqué designs depicting men, beasts and birds.

Except at night and in foul weather, the tents were mainly the domain of the women. The men spent most of their waking hours outside—almost constantly on horseback—tending their herds or hunting hare, boar, deer and other wild creatures. Such sport no doubt kept their archery skills keen, and the game so obtained provided a welcome supplement to their staple diet of mutton, beef and horse flesh cooked in great cauldrons. Sometimes the Scythians prepared a sort of haggis by boiling the flesh of a cow in its own skin. They could vary their fare with fish from the prolific rivers that traversed their domain. They loved cheeses, too, but above all they relished the sharp, slightly intoxicating drink called kumiss: made from fermented mare's milk, it is still popular among the herdsmen of Central Asia and Mongolia.

Although their horse herds were enormous, providing food, drink, hides and personal transport, not every horse was considered a proper mount. The Scythians rode only geldings. Since they kept their herds on the open range, they had to castrate all the stallions but those needed for breeding; otherwise every male horse would have cut out his own group of females and galloped off with them.

At the time of their zenith, in the Fifth and Fourth centuries B.C., the Scythians were composed of at least four mounted tribes. The strongest dominated the choice pasturage and provided leadership in time of war. Herodotus names the four—the Auchatae, the Catiari, the Traspians and the Paralatae—and distinguishes the last as foremost, calling the tribe the Royal Scythians. He and other alien observers described its chief as a king because of his wealth, elaborate trappings and prestige.

The Scythian tribes had neighbors whom Herodotus went to great lengths to describe, no doubt coloring the facts with legend. Along the sea south of the Scythians lived the Tauri, a gloomy people said to exist entirely by warfare and plunder, who sacrificed shipwreck victims to a virgin goddess. Ranged across the steppe north of the Scythians were a number of other folk equally notorious in one way or another. Among them were the Agathyrsi, who practiced promiscuous intercourse "so that they may all be brothers and, as members of one family, may neither envy nor hate one another." The Neurians, so their neighbors swore, once a year turned into wolves for a few days. (Here is the earliest-known record of the werewolf myth.) The Androphagi, or Man-Eaters, were reputed to be cannibals. The Budini—a powerful people with bright red hair and deep blue eyes—and their compatriots, the Geloni, would periodically engage in wild drunken revels. Herodotus also mentioned Thrace, a country of barbarians neighboring Scythia on the west, and he described in some detail the Sarmatians, a nomadic people akin to the Scythians in customs, art and language, who lived on the steppe east of the Don and who were to play a crucial role in the Scythians' future.

Whatever the effect such neighbors may have had on them, the Scythian tribes retained their own identity. To make administration easier, their entire domain—what the Greeks called Scythia—was divided into four districts. A governor kept the peace in each district and saw to the collection of taxes from the settled farmers of the steppe and from the lands bordering it. He also oversaw and encouraged trading operations in the Greek colonies along the Black Sea. At the threat of war, the Scythians cooperated with one another in matters of recruitment and strategy. The hordes of warriors raised during a crisis served without pay except for their food and clothing and a share of the booty. The last was divided according to the number of enemies a man killed—the proof of which was provided by their severed heads.

Though the Scythians gave the appearance of tribal unity when it came to war with outsiders, they were not quite a nation. It seems likely that the tribes fought among themselves over grasslands or cattle. A tribe suffering drought on its own range might be moved to violate the pasturage of another, or a tribe whose herd had been reduced by disease might steal the cattle of a neighboring tribe. The Soviet archeologist Sergei Ivanovich Rudenko has pointed out that, up to a century ago, among nomadic peoples "driving off cattle was not regarded as a felony and rustling was considered a special kind of profession."

In spite of such internal skirmishing, the Scythians were united by custom and a common language. A mere sprinklet of their words survives in Herodotus. According to him, *pata* meant "to kill"; *spou* meant "eye"; *arima,* "one"; *oior,* "man"; and the word *arimaspi* referred to a legendary race of one-eyed people. Such words are enough, however, for philologists to say that the Scythians spoke a dialect descended from the prehistoric Indo-European language from which the major tongues of the Western world have evolved. And since theirs was a nonliterate society, oral traditions, rather than written law, bound them together and perpetuated their culture.

Like many of the other nomadic tribes inhabiting the vast Eurasian steppes, the Scythians were tra-ditionally polygamous. A wealthy Scythian could take several wives, and upon his death a son or a brother would assume them as his own. Thus their families tended to grow very large and sprawl into intricate and overlapping clans knit together not only by common beliefs but also by complex entanglements of blood and kinship. Moreover, chiefs were given to taking wives from among alien people as well as from their own or other Scythian tribes.

Thus the tribe functioned as a kind of melting pot. Outsiders could melt in, but the reverse was severely frowned upon. The tribe showed its hostility to alien customs in direct ways. There was, for example, a king named Scyles. No one minded his marrying a Greek woman, although he already had a Scythian wife. But then Scyles took to spending more and more time in the city of Olbia and became too fond of Greek ways, finally going so far as to take part in a riotous celebration to an alien deity, the Greek wine god, Dionysus. His Scythian relatives heard of it —and a half brother murdered him.

If tribal custom was sacred, it was also bloody. Warriors not only cut off the heads of slain enemies —occasionally even of kinsmen—but traditionally made leather-bound drinking cups from the skulls of their most detested foes. Wealthier warriors lined these grisly trophies with gold and proudly displayed them to impress honored visitors.

On the battlefield the Scythians also took the scalps of slain enemies, and Herodotus tells in horrifying detail what they did with them. "The Scythian soldier," he wrote, "scrapes the scalp clean of flesh and, softening it by rubbing between the hands, uses it thenceforth as a napkin. The Scyth is proud of these scalps and hangs them from his bridle rein; the great-

Bands of Turkoman nomads gather with their mounts near the town of Morsian in northern Afghanistan to observe a tradition that goes back to the first horsemen—an annual get-together, celebrated with feasting and games. The reed mats afford some protection against the biting wind.

Adorned with gold, bones of a young Scythian woman lie as discovered in 1971 beneath a 35-foot-high burial mound in the Ukraine. Wearing a purple gown stitched with 200 gold plaques, she was laid to rest 2,400 years ago on a carpet-covered plank. On her arms were three gold bracelets and on her fingers 11 rings. Under her left shoulder was a bronze mirror.

er the number of such napkins that a man can show, the more highly is he esteemed among them. Many make themselves cloaks by sewing a quantity of these scalps together. . . . Such are the Scythian customs with respect to scalps."

Blood often flowed freely in Scythian rituals. The neophyte warrior was expected to drink some of the blood of his first fallen foe. Parties to an alliance would seal their pact with a blood oath, letting their blood into a bowl of wine, dipping their knives or javelins or other weapons into it and drinking the mix. Blood sacrifices, commonly of horses and cattle, were made to a small pantheon headed by a goddess called Tabiti, roughly comparable to the Greek Hestia, goddess of fire and the hearth. Humans were sacrificed only sparingly; one prisoner of each hundred taken in battle was given to a god of war, represented by an iron sword planted atop a mound of brushwood.

Other than the mound of brush with its symbolic sword, the Scythians had no temples or altars or religious images, and evidently no priests as such. Soothsayers, however, abounded among them and included in their ranks eunuchoid or effeminate males called *enarees*—a word that meant "men-women" or "halfmen." The *enarees* were supposedly paying a penalty inflicted on their ancestors by Aphrodite, the Greek goddess of love, whose temple they had plundered while rampaging through western Asia. The *enarees* themselves referred to their condition as "the female sickness," and Herodotus in his discussion of them says, "Travelers who visit Scythia can see what sort of disease it is."

Some soothsayers foretold the future with willow wands that they positioned on the ground; others prophesied by furling and unfurling strips of linden

bark. Like the shamans of North American Indian tribes, the soothsayers probably managed their divinations by self-induced ecstatic fits.

The soothsayers were greatly feared, and part of that fear grew out of their power to execute tribal law. For instance, it appears that the thoughts of men were held to have enough force to cause the sickness of a chief. Thus, when a Scythian chief became sick, his illness was always attributed to the disloyalty of some tribesman who had sworn a false oath in the presence of the leader. In such a crisis soothsayers would be summoned to identify the culprit. Once accused, the tribesman would be summarily beheaded —except in the rare event that other seers agreed to hear an appeal and exonerated him. The soothsayers had sound cause to stick together, since they divided the property of tribesmen they condemned. On the other hand, a seer who was found guilty by his peers of false identification would be bound, placed in a wagon full of brushwood and burned to death.

Scythian women had little power—magical or otherwise—beyond the confines of their households. Their status differed sharply from that of females in most contemporary tribes of mounted nomads. For example, among the Sarmatians who dominated the steppe region east of the Don River, women not only rode but fought with the men. (Indeed, the ways of the Sarmatian women led the Greeks to believe that they were descendants of the legendary Amazons.) In contrast, Scythian women traveled in carts or wagons instead of on horseback, and were relieved of much of the common toil of nomadic life. Some scholars surmise that at one time the women may have lived a more active and influential life, but as the Scythians rose to eminence and accumulated great

wealth they gradually developed something similar to the Moslem and Hindu purdah system, in which women are secluded.

To spare their women drudgery, the Scythians kept captives of war as slaves. These they would often blind and assign to the milking of mares and the churning of kumiss. Herodotus related a legend that told how once, when the Scythian warriors were long absent from home, their women took the slaves to bed and spawned a new generation that the warriors had to defeat on their return. After much struggle with these interlopers, the Scythians laid down their weapons and took up their horsewhips. "So long as they see us with arms in our hands," one of them said, "they imagine themselves our equals in birth and bravery. But let them behold us with no other weapon but the whip, and they will feel they are our slaves, and flee before us." The strategy worked, and "the slaves were so astounded that they forgot to fight and immediately ran away."

In this male-dominated society, the warriors and chieftains were revered, honored in death as well as in life. Even the loss of a common warrior entailed a period of preburial mourning and feasting during which the embalmed corpse was hauled by wagon among the friends of the deceased. But at the death of a king all Scythian tribes joined in a show of stupendous grief that lasted 40 days (*pages 117-121*). Men of the dominant tribe, the Royal Scythians, would crop their hair, lacerate their ears, foreheads, noses and arms, and stick arrows through their left hands. These mutilations would be matched by other tribesmen as the king's body—stuffed with a preparation of chopped cypress, frankincense, parsley seed and anise seed—was hauled from tribe to tribe toward

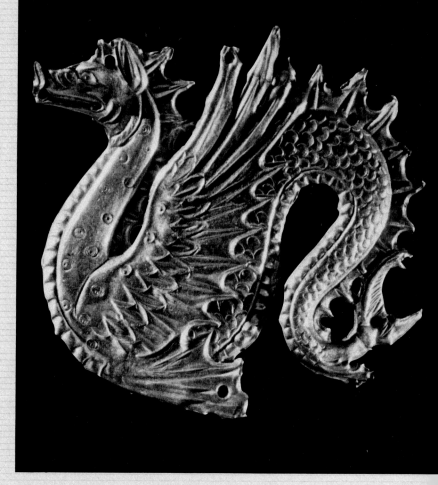

The Scythians' love of flashy ornaments led them to decorate their finest clothing with plaques like these of hammered or molded gold, the biggest of which measures no more than two inches long. The plaques took a variety of shapes, ranging from geometric designs (ornamented triangle, below right) and abstractions (bird's head, far right, middle) to human forms and imaginary animals. The winged creature below is a hippocampus—a sea monster with a horselike head and a fish's tail; it was made by a Fourth Century B.C. Greek artisan.

the burial place in an ever-increasing procession.

There the king would be laid in his grave under a thatched canopy with the best of all his weapons and possessions. Then the funeral party would strangle one of his concubines, his cupbearer, his cook, his lackey, his messenger and his best horses—sometimes scores of them—and place all the bodies by him. After covering the grave with an enormous mound, perhaps 60 feet high, the tribesmen would feast, and then erect small tents in which they purified themselves in the heady vapors given off by smoldering hemp seeds.

Even then, the funeral was not always over. One year later as many as 50 Scythian youths might be selected from among those who had directly served the king. They, too, would be strangled, embalmed and pierced lengthwise with a stake so they could be set astride an equal number of embalmed and impaled horses arranged in a circle around the new royal tomb. Presumably these sacrifices served as an eerie guard to scare away grave robbers. Whatever its purpose, such a custom must have provided those close to the king with a strong motive for working to assure his health, safety and longevity.

For all his detailed accounts of Scythian customs, Herodotus declares that they were "not such as I admire." But there was one custom in which the Scythians seemed to him to be "wiser than any nation upon the face of the earth": their way of war and, particularly, the wily way in which they handled Darius the Great of Persia when he came conquering in 514 B.C. In his reports Herodotus has no time for legend or hearsay, but bases his description on hard, historical facts.

At that time the Persian Empire was at its height,

with twin capitals at Persepolis and Susa. Coveting Greece as his ultimate prize, Darius led an enormous expedition over the Bosporus, which he crossed on a bridge of boats. But before invading Greece he decided first to subdue the Scythians, presumably to prevent them from attacking him from the north. To do this he had to cross the Danube, spanning it with another bridge of boats. He informed the commander of the Danube bridge that he expected to bring the Scythians to heel within 60 days.

The Scythians had other ideas. They quickly saw they would have no chance alone in a direct encounter with an invading force of 700,000 men. They sent envoys to ask help of all the neighboring peoples —the gloomy Tauri, the promiscuous Agathyrsi, the werewolf Neuri, the lawless Man-Eaters, the hard-drinking, red-haired Budini and their friends the Geloni. They also sent a request for reinforcements to the Sarmatian nomads east of the Don. When only the Sarmatians, the Geloni and the Budini pledged help, the Scythians determined to avoid any pitched battle. They settled on an evasive strategy and divided their warriors into two divisions: an elite force of Scythians commanded by a chieftain named Idanthyrsus, which would be joined by the Geloni and the Budini, and a second that would be made up of the Sarmatians and the rest of the Scythians. Scythian families, loaded into their wagons, headed north under orders to keep moving. Then, as the divisions dispersed, the fleetest Scythian horsemen were dispatched to make contact with the Persians.

When he sighted the Scythian patrol, Darius had come three days' march from the Danube. Instantly he lunged in pursuit. And so began one of the longest and most futile chases in military annals. The swift patrol baited Darius into pursuit of the elite Scythian force under Idanthyrsus. And with that, the rough horsemen of the steppe toyed with the Persian army.

Darius would lunge and the Scythians would recede like a mirage, leaving behind burned pasture and ruined wells. The Persians marched ever onward— enormous columns encumbered with foot soldiers, chariots and the paraphernalia of highly organized conventional combat. Idanthyrsus took care to stay just a day's march in front. He snipped at the Persian flanks, picked off stragglers, hounded Darius with sudden glancing raids at night. By day he and his Scythians danced ever on the horizon. Darius did not own a horse that could sniff their dust.

Idanthyrsus led Darius on day by day, week after week, through prairies and across rivers, into the woods and out. He led him maliciously into the lands of the Man-Eaters and the Neuri, who had refused to join in the Scythian alliance. He led him in circles, and once again into the Scythians' own steppe domain. The Persians grew fatigued, riddled with sickness. On the burned land, foraging for food was itself a consuming struggle.

It seemed to Darius a very strange war. There was nothing to be captured and held—no cities, no buildings, no plunder, nothing but the rimless steppe. He was fighting air. The Persian, moreover, was afflicted with the civilized disease of valor. He could not grasp why his quarry would not stand and fight for the sake of sheer honor. At last he sent a plaintive query to Idanthyrsus: "Strange man, why do you keep on flying before me?" He alluded to himself as their lord and naïvely ordered the Scythians either to stand and fight or send tributes signifying surrender. Idanthyrsus, with infuriating insolence, replied, "In return for

Among the jewelry buried during the
Fourth Century B.C. in tombs north
of the Crimea near Kakhovka were these
gold earrings. The one at left features
a pair of ducks, the other a woman
—perhaps a goddess—seated on a lamb.

Found in another Crimean tomb was
this colorful glass necklace. Scholars
speculate that it may have originated
in the Caucasus or in Greek colonies
on the Black Sea, where it came by
trade to its delighted Scythian owner.

calling yourself my lord, I say to you: 'Go weep.' "

Time was running out for Darius. One day he looked up to behold an array of advancing Scythian horsemen. Now at last the battle for which he lusted was at hand. Suddenly the Scythians thundered across the plain, but not toward him. It was a very puzzling maneuver, accompanied by shouts of merriment and jubilation. What did this mean? Darius was told by an aide that the Scythian army—there within sight of the mighty Persians—had spotted a hare and given chase.

"These men do indeed despise us utterly," said Darius, and forthwith decided to retreat by night, leaving behind as decoys his sick and wounded and some asses, whose braying might deceive the Scythians into supposing his army was still at hand.

So while Darius returned to Asia to prepare for his war on Greece, the Scythians prevailed on the south Russian steppe. They outlasted not only Darius but the Persian Empire itself. In the Fourth Century B.C. they expanded westward until Philip of Macedon, the father of Alexander the Great, drove them back from the Danube after a battle in which the Scythian king Ateas, then aged 90 or more, was killed. A few years later, in about 336 B.C., Alexander himself, having conquered Thrace and before heading for further conquests in Asia, dispatched his Thracian governor, Zepyrion, to discipline the nomads further. The Scythians killed Zepyrion, routed his troops and set up outposts in the Balkans before returning home.

But something new and ominous had begun to happen in their homeland. The Scythians, under long Greek influence, had become urbanized and sedentary. By contrast, the Sarmatians, who had helped them against Darius, were waxing powerful and pressing westward. By 346 B.C. the Sarmatians had crossed their traditional border, the Don, and unrelentingly continued their westward push. Thus, even though the Scythians were to remain prosperous and powerful throughout the Fourth Century B.C., a circle was inexorably closing in upon them. In another 200 years the first horsemen to have ridden into recorded history would be scattered—and the wildest of them, like the horses they rode, would be tamed.

A Priceless Legacy in Gold and Silver

The mounted horsemen of the south Russian steppe known as the Scythians, whose detailed record was set down in the Fifth Century B.C. by Herodotus, awed their contemporaries with their ferocious gusto. Their habit of drinking wine undiluted impressed even the Spartans, who, when they wanted to imbibe stronger wine than was customary, gave the order that vessels be filled "Scythian fashion." Indeed, the Spartans attributed the madness of one of their leaders not to some supernatural cause, but to the fact that he was in the habit of drinking like a Scythian.

In keeping with the exuberance of their character, the Scythians loved lavish objects: gold and silver cups, amphorae, vases and jewelry, decorated with images of themselves *(below)* and made for them by craftsmen living in Greek towns on the Black Sea or in Greece itself. Of incalculable value as works of art, these glittering masterpieces provide, as the following examples from Soviet museums demonstrate, a lively glimpse of a distinctive people at work, at play and at war.

Only four inches high, a Fourth Century B.C. loving cup found in a tomb at Gaimonov, north of the Crimea, features two long-haired warriors with weapons and wearing clothing typical of the Scythians. Their faces and hands are wrought of silver and their garments of gold.

Wranglers of the Steppe

One of the most beautiful of all Scythian discoveries is the Fourth Century B.C. wine holder below, uncovered in 1862 at Chertomlyk on the Dnieper River. It is also the one piece that provides the most intimate glimpse of the Scythians' deep involvement with their compact, well-muscled horses. The relatively small size of their mounts enabled the Scythians—who rode without stirrups—to hang on easily. Herds of these animals under their control must have been enormous: at Ulski, east of the Black Sea, 400 of the best could be spared for burial with a single chieftain.

In this detail from the amphora, a Scythian prepares to throw a newly captured horse.

Three men strain against a bucking horse; the ropes they once held have been lost.

Three sieved spouts filtered sediment from the wine kept in this 28-inch-high gold and silver amphora. Each of the holes could be stoppered with a bung.

After being saddled and bridled, a mount waits patiently as its rider undoes the hobbles that kept it from wandering in the night.

Pastoral Chores and Wild Fantasies

An excavation in 1971, at Tovsta in the Ukraine, brought to light this spectacular gold pectoral, which weighs a full two and a half pounds. It was made for a Scythian client, during the Fourth Century B.C., by a Greek master smith. He managed to cram into its 12-inch diameter an exquisitely detailed picture of the Scythians and the animals with which their lives were interwoven. Nothing in nature escaped the eye of the artist, from the muscle-tensed bodies of the nomads to the tiniest grasshoppers. He cast single parts separately and soldered each one to twisted cords of gold.

Forty-four golden animals adorn the pectoral. On its inner band, cows, ewes and mares tenderly suckle their young; a horse scratches itself. At the center, two Scythians cooperate in the making of a garment (detailed below). The middle band, with its floral design, was once inlaid with enamel; bits of it still cling to the flowers. One of the predominant themes of Scythian art—battling animals both actual and imaginary—fills the outer band.

Two men kneel to sew a sheepskin with needle and thread. Each keeps his gorytus—bow and arrow case—close at hand in case of danger.

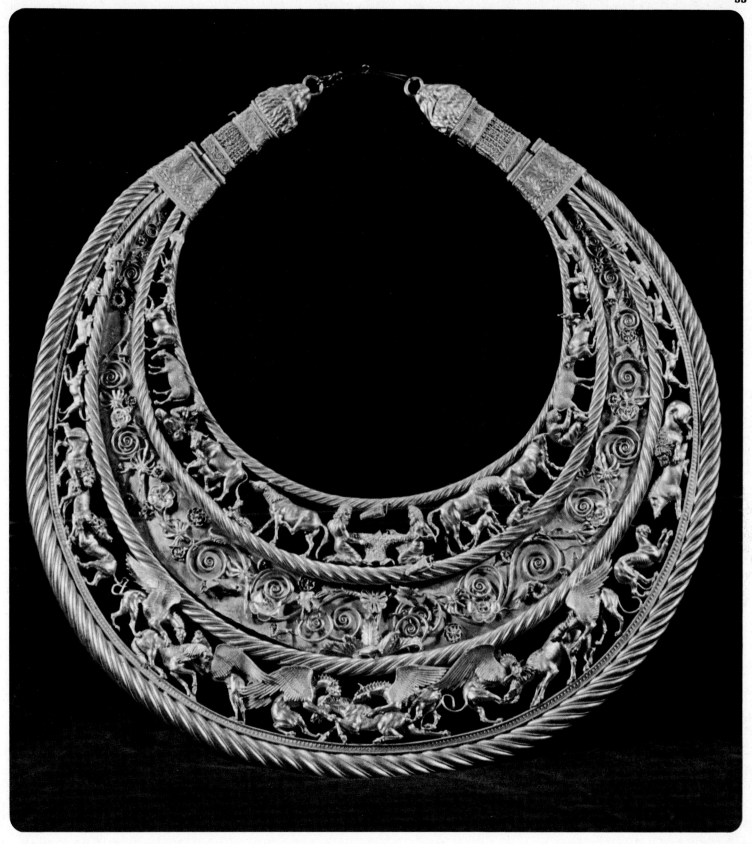

The Bonds of Brotherhood

The 2,400-year-old vase below, dug out of a Scythian grave in 1875, sheds light on the horsemen's behavior. Fierce though their reputation may have been among their neighbors on the steppes and among the Medians and the Assyrians to the south, the Scythians were, as the scenes at right clearly reveal, solicitous of one another's welfare.

A proud, self-willed people, ready to extort from others what they needed to survive, they may have led far more peaceful lives among themselves than history has allowed. As stockbreeders, they spent most of their days under the open sky, engaged in an endless round of chores connected with their horses, their herds of cattle and their flocks of sheep.

An elegantly wrought vase from Kul Oba in the Crimea, five inches high and made of electrum—an alloy of gold and silver—depicts Scythians involved in a number of comradely activities.

One nomad probes another's mouth in search of an aching tooth. Their trousers are decorated—perhaps with the gold plaques that the Scythians sometimes wore sewn to their clothes.

Wearing a distinctive pointed hood and tunic, a bearded Scythian carefully dresses a friend's wounded leg. Attached to his belt, as ever within easy reach, is his decorated gorytus.

Sharpening Skills on the Hunt

The Fourth Century B.C. cup below commemorates one of the Scythians' best-loved activities—hunting. The grasslands and river valleys through which the horsemen roamed supported a wide range of wild animals, which included deer, boars, foxes, wolves and, as the scene at right vividly demonstrates, even lions.

When they hunted such beasts, the Scythians were perfecting their skills with spear and bow and arrow. But they also valued the meat and pelts thus obtained. Herodotus claimed that they cut open the animal and took out the bones, then placed the meat in cauldrons or in the animal's own paunch and cooked it over fires fueled with the fatty bones, a substitute for wood on the treeless steppe.

This five-inch-high cup with attached handles, from a tomb at Solokha in the Ukraine, is crafted of gilded silver.

Aided by dogs that look rather like modern borzois, a hunter draws back his arm to drive his spear into a wounded lion. His dress proclaims him a Scythian, but his beardless face is more typical of the Greek ideal youth, a favorite subject in classical art.

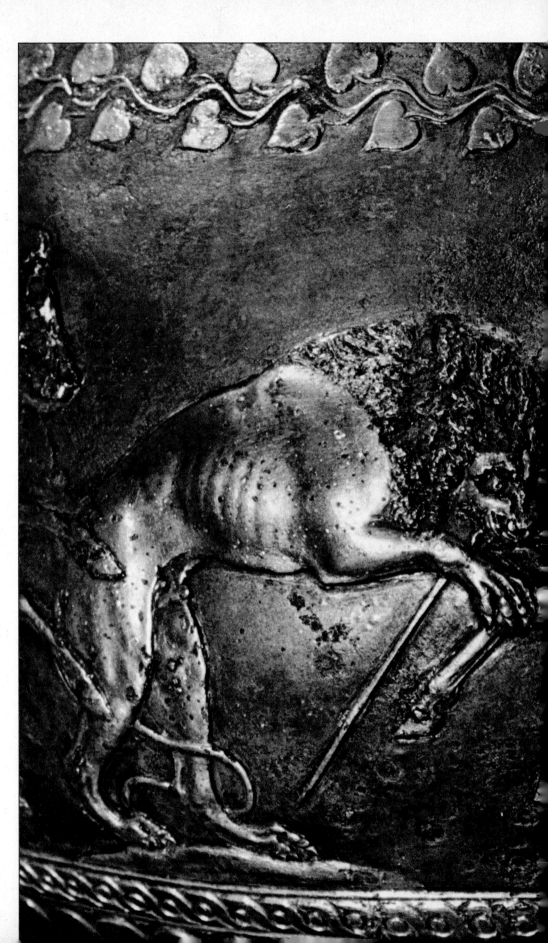

Fearless Warriors on the Battlefield

A gold comb seems an unlikely object for the depiction of a life-death struggle, and yet that is what decorates the comb shown below—a Fourth Century B.C. treasure from Solokha.

The Scythians were great fighters, and regularly worshiped a god of war. To honor him, they sacrificed one of every hundred prisoners, bleeding the victim to death and cutting off his right hand and arm, which they hurled into the air. "Then the other victims are slain," wrote Herodotus. "Those who have offered the sacrifice depart, leaving the hands and arms where they may chance to have fallen."

This gold comb was discovered in the grave of a man who had probably worn it as a decoration in his long hair.

Although the three bearded warriors are obviously Scythians, the Greek goldsmith who made the four-inch-wide comb added some Greek elements to his work, including the helmets, the armor and possibly the shields.

The Scythians thundered into history as masters of the horse, but they were clearly its creatures as well. The horse gave them not only their unprecedented mobility but also their brash outlook on the world; once they perfected the technique of riding, they —and others like them on the steppes—were transformed from plodding nomadic herdsmen into a conspicuous and audacious host.

The transformation came as the culmination of an immensely long evolutionary process that got underway at least 60 million years ago, when man did not yet exist and the horse, if it could be considered that at all, stood 12 inches at the shoulders—about the size of a fox. This improbable ancestor of today's *Equus caballus* is known as *Hyracotherium*, and its fossil remains, dating from the epoch of geologic history known as the Eocene, have been turned up by paleontologists in places as far-flung as England, France, Wyoming, Utah and New Mexico.

Hyracotherium had an arched back, a rather short neck and muzzle, and short-crowned teeth devoid of the hard covering that protects those of its modern descendants. Its padded, doglike foot was strikingly different from the basic five-toed mammalian extremity: there were four toes on each front limb and three on each hind one. Moreover, each toe was tipped, prophetically, with a tiny hoof, still little more than a nail or claw.

"Judging from the assemblage of animals that lived

Two bearded riders, each an inch and a half high, on golden mounts, seem to leap from the ends of a torque (shown fully, inset) found encircling the neck of a chieftain in a Fourth Century B.C. grave in the Crimea. Woven of six gold strands bound in an intricate sheath inlaid with enamel, the torque was made by a Greek craftsman familiar with Scythian ways.

at the time of *Hyracotherium*, and also from the nature of the deposits in which these fossils are found," say paleontologists Hildegarde Howard and Chester Stock, the authors of *The Ascent of Equus*, "the little fellows were forest dwellers, frequenting, perhaps, the banks of streams and lakes where they fed upon tender-leafed shrubs." These experts have concluded that "there is little to suggest to the casual observer that *Hyracotherium* was a horse."

Certainly any modern race-track habitué who might have been privileged to observe *Hyracotherium*—or *Eohippus*, the dawn horse, as it is also called—would not have been seriously tempted to bet that this little animal would, in time, grow up to be the heroic steed evoked in the Book of Job:

"The glory of his nostrils is terrible. He paweth in the valley, and rejoiceth in his strength: he goeth on to meet the armed man. He mocketh at fear, and is not affrighted; neither turneth he back from the sword. The quiver rattleth against him, the glittering spear and shield. He swalloweth the ground with fierceness and rage: neither believeth he that it is the sound of the trumpet. He saith among the trumpets, Ha, ha! and he smelleth the battle from afar off, the thunder of the captains, and the shouting."

Such was *Hyracotherium*'s destined role, and the dawn horse was off and running toward that future. By the time it rounded the curve of the Oligocene epoch some 40 million years ago, its kind was extinct in Europe, and for a long span thereafter the evolution of the horse would take place on the North American continent, where *Hyracotherium* continued to flourish.

During the Oligocene the climate changed to become more markedly seasonal, and as the environment underwent modification so did the ancestral horse. Warm, damp forests began to give way to grassy plains. Adapted to forest conditions, the many-toed feet of *Hyracotherium* had provided support on spongy ground, but now another accommodation was required to equip the dawn horse for a life on the firmer ground and open terrain of the plains (page 46). Before the end of the Oligocene, a descendant of *Hyracotherium* called *Mesohippus* and a later one, *Miohippus,* had lost the fourth toe on both front feet—and the middle toe on all four feet had grown markedly bigger than the outer toes. The new conformation made running on the plains easier. *Miohippus,* moreover, outstripped all its predecessors in size. Its legs had lengthened, raising the animal to a stately height of two feet: six hands at the withers, as its descendants would ultimately be measured, with a hand equaling four inches. Not only were its legs and toes becoming increasingly specialized for swift flight over hard surfaces in order to escape predators, but also its neck and head had lengthened to permit grazing on grass, instead of browsing on the foliage of bushes.

There were also major changes inside *Miohippus'* mouth. Its teeth were evolving in a way that would ultimately allow the horse to consume harsh grasses without damage from gritty abrasives taken in with the food. This indispensable adaptation has several important features. Hard enamel contoured in intricate patterns encloses the dentine of the so-called cheek teeth. Cement coats and helps to protect the enamel, welding the crown into a solid unit. Crowns of striking length—two to three inches—extend deep into the jaws below the gum line, and bone forming beneath the roots continually pushes out reserve crown as grinding wears away the upper surface. The front teeth, used for cropping or chopping, are shorter than the cheek teeth and are coated with a single layer of enamel and cement.

All these specializations—of teeth, legs, neck and head—advanced dramatically beginning some 20 million years ago, in the Miocene epoch. By then, the horse called *Merychippus* possessed greatly enlarged middle toes and vestigial outer ones that only touched the ground when the animal was in flight and pounding hard. It also had teeth that could chop and reduce vegetation much tougher than the tender forest herbage on which *Hyracotherium* had grazed. Moreover, its head had further lengthened, enabling *Merychippus* to feed easily on the low-growing grasses of the plains where it lived.

But not until 10 million years later, in the late Miocene, did the first one-toed ancestral horses appear. Two groups—*Pliohippus* and *Dinohippus*—displayed relatively minor differences in anatomy from the modern animal. Still, eight million more years had to elapse before the hoofed creature classed as *Equus* —the true horse—emerged in the Pleistocene epoch along with *Homo sapiens*—man.

Before the onset of the last ice age, *Equus* flourished in North and South America. As advancing glaciers brought bitter cold and reduced the amount of pasturage, herds of horses were crossing into the forests and plains of Asia and Europe over the land bridge that rose and fell in what is now the Bering Strait. The horses that stayed behind in the New World survived until about 10,000 or 11,000 years ago, and then inexplicably died off. Students of the modern horse's lineage thus consider the migrants from America as the direct ancestors of the wild horse that ultimately entered partnership with man.

Starting 50,000 years ago, these forebears of today's horse spread across northern Asia and Europe, and spawned several varieties of horses. They evolved into two broad types: one with massive bones, a long skull and prominent face; the second with a slender frame and shorter snout. Neanderthal and Cro-Magnon men knew both animals well—as food. At Solutré in France, for example, what appears to have been a kill site used by many generations of Cro-Magnon hunters has yielded the accumulated bones of perhaps 10,000 wild horses that hunters presumably stampeded over a cliff.

Additional striking evidence of the importance of the horse to hunters during the Upper Paleolithic is its frequent appearance in drawings on the walls of caves in France and northern Spain—at Combarelles, Lascaux, Altamira and elsewhere. The creatures depicted by Cro-Magnon artists often bear a noticeable resemblance to the wild horses that survived on the steppes of eastern Europe and Central Asia into modern times—the shaggy tarpan and the Roman-nosed Przewalski (pages 50-51). But, though early men seemed to admire the horse, rendering it with grace in their art, they continued to know it as they knew the bison, the reindeer and the wild ox (called the aurochs), as a beast to be killed and devoured.

The taming of the horse had to await the "taming" of man, which began with the rise of agriculture and a settled way of life in the Near East some 9,000 or 10,000 years ago—and then only after the domestication of sheep, goats and cattle. When at last man became a keeper of horses, they served him for a long time only as a source of meat and milk and hides.

The riding of the horse, the achievement that was to signal a point of demarcation in man's ancient ways, was still far in the future.

The earliest evidence of the domestication of the horse comes not from the Near East but from that steppe region now known as the Ukraine. Here the bones of horses have turned up along with other animal remains in the garbage heaps of neolithic farmers and early pastoralists, who emerged on the steppe during the Fourth Millennium B.C.

The growing importance of the horse to the farmers is suggested by the steady decline in the remains of game in their refuse piles and by a growing preponderance of horse bones. Then, around the turn of the Second Millennium, the archeological record breaks off. Evidently under pressure from other peoples intruding into their domain, the farmers of the Ukrainian steppe exchanged their settled way of life for a seminomadic one. They may well have begun using horses as pack animals when moving camp, and toward the end of their sedentary existence may have hitched them to carts. There is a possibility also that they sometimes sat astride the quieter horses they were taking to pasture—though if they rode at all, it is more likely that they climbed aboard their docile, more predictable cattle.

It is the popular but mistaken view today that since the horse is the best and most "natural" animal to ride, it must have been the first. This notion has nurtured the judgment that riding animals other than horses is quaint or exotic. In ancient times the reverse was the case. Horses were not even used as draft animals until after other animals had been hitched to wheeled carts. In the Near East, where the art of domestication first burgeoned and the wheel

An Equine Genealogy

Some 60 million years ago, *Hyracotherium* (also known as *Eohippus*), an animal no bigger than a fox, nibbled the foliage of the swampy forests of Europe and America. Though the species died out in Europe, in North America it began to evolve into the swift, grass-eating animal of the plains: *Equus*, the horse. Through the ages, descendants of *Hyracotherium* emigrated to Asia when a land bridge linked the two continents; in time, all horses became extinct in America. The only wild Eurasian horse to survive today is *Equus przewalskii*, whose ancestors were also forebears of the modern horse.

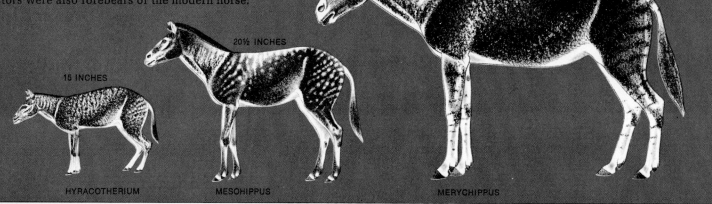

15 INCHES

20½ INCHES

35 INCHES

HYRACOTHERIUM

MESOHIPPUS

MERYCHIPPUS

Size and foot structure are the most noticeable differences between the skeletons of Hyracotherium and Equus, but there are other distinctions as important. Equus' backbone was not arched, and the vertebrae at the withers had developed long spines to which were attached tendons strong enough to hold the long neck and the heavy skull with its large, grass-grinding teeth. The lengthened neck let the horse eat without bending its legs, which, structurally and muscularly, were adapted for swift running.

HYRACOTHERIUM

EQUUS

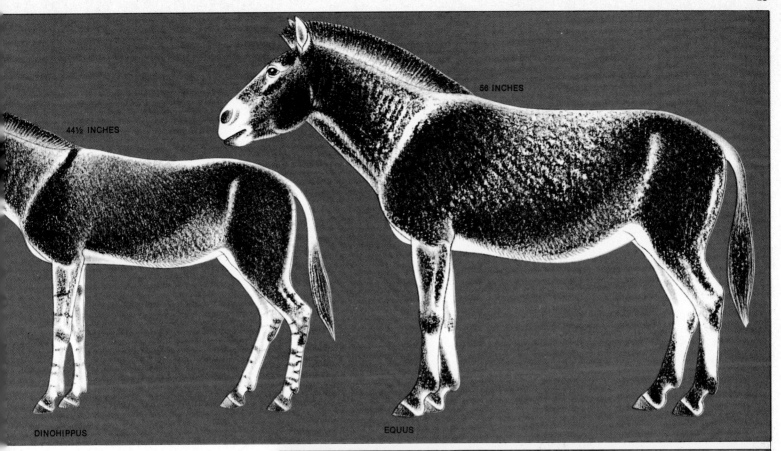

44½ INCHES

56 INCHES

DINOHIPPUS

EQUUS

Scaled reconstructions (above) of the horse's ancestors chart major evolutionary steps from little Hyracotherium to Equus przewalskii. Mesohippus, which evolved from Hyracotherium 35 million years ago, began to develop the longer, stronger legs that were to make the horse such a fast runner. Over a seven-million-year period, Merychippus grew leggier and its side toes became smaller. Dinohippus (10 to 5 million years ago) was one of the first one-toed horses, and Equus, the first with true hoofs.

Splayed Foot to Compact Hoof

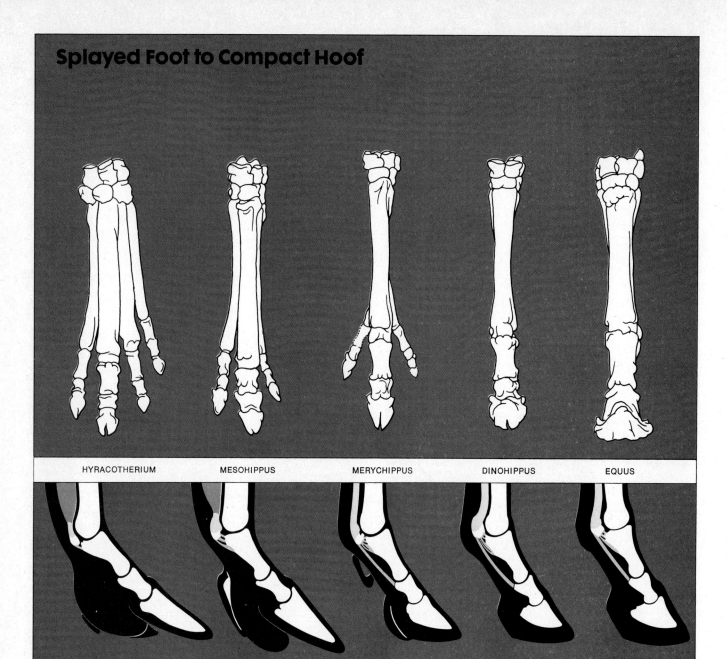

HYRACOTHERIUM   MESOHIPPUS   MERYCHIPPUS   DINOHIPPUS   EQUUS

The horse bears its weight on a single, central digit on each foot. These drawings explain how the splayed and padded foot of Hyracotherium changed in three ways to become the compact, hard hoof of the modern horse. All the toes except the central digit gradually became vestigial and then vanished, leaving the horse, in effect, on tiptoe, ready to take flight. At the same time, the soft pad disappeared so that only the nail, or hoof, came into contact with the ground. The foot muscles (pink) vanished as the foot lengthened, and the horse came to rely on the elastic properties of foot tendons and ligaments (blue and yellow) to give it an efficient bounding motion; as a result it could run tirelessly across the plains in flight from predators.

originated, there were at first no horses to use for hauling. Instead the civilized peoples inhabiting the Tigris-Euphrates Valley in Mesopotamia relied on the ox and a variety of ass called the onager; the ox was directed by voice and goad, and both animals lent themselves to control by a nose ring.

The horse apparently came to the Near East around 2000 B.C., and as something new and strange, it was known as "the ass of the mountain." Some scholars think it was brought there by herdsmen from lands to the north, or perhaps that it was acquired through trade. Presumably herdsmen had learned to use horses to pull sledges or light carts and to control the animals by a noseband—a thong or a rope extending around the nose and under the chin, and held in place by a strap that went behind the horse's ears. A nose ring that successfully guided the movements of oxen and onagers would have induced outright panic in a creature as high-strung as the horse.

The horse's nature obviously had a lot to do with its initial failure to attract riders. Few men would have been tempted to mount so unpredictable a beast —and fewer still would have been able to stay aboard. Little *Hyracotherium* had evolved into the most temperamental of all domestic animals, able to elude predators by its sheer speed—the only possible defense on terrain that offered no place to hide. In body and mind the horse is perfectly designed for flight, not fight. The horse relies on its uncommonly keen eyesight and marvelously acute sense of smell to send it galloping off at any hint of danger. Yet, once trapped, it kicks, bucks, slashes out with its forefeet and bites—often lethally. Also, stallions protecting mares and foals will attack.

Perhaps most important, the untamed horse is nat-urally likely to go all but berserk when *anything* lands on its back, simply because it has learned through the millennia that *anything* is likely to be a predator. Thus, even if man had dreamed of riding the horse much earlier than he did, he could hardly have expected a hospitable reception from the animal that one day would become his partner.

Even tamed, the horse retains a temperament that cannot be dallied with. Its psychology "is difficult to construe with any pretense to exactitude," says Dr. J. F. Ryff, an authority on the animal. "It is at once timid and courageous, affectionate and unfriendly, docile and ungovernable, hot-headed and phlegmatic, teachable and obtuse."

Some observers believe that a horse is never truly tamed so much as temporarily conditioned. An example that lends strong support to such thinking comes from the *Memoirs of the Crusades,* written by Jean, Sire de Joinville, a nobleman who accompanied King Louis IX of France to the Holy Land in the 13th Century A.D.

According to Joinville, the Christian and Saracen armies were encamped opposite each other at Damietta in Egypt, and the Saracens were constantly charging the French camp. "Now it happened that my Lord Walter of Autrèche . . . mounted upon his horse, with his shield at his neck and his helmet on his head . . . stuck spurs into his horse to ride against the Turks. . . . But it so chanced that [the moment] he came up to the Turks he fell, and his horse flew over his body; and the horse went on . . . to our enemies, because the Saracens were for the most part mounted on mares, for which reason the Lord Walter's horse drew to the side of the Saracens."

In light of the horse's mercurial disposition, its

One of man's earliest portrayals of the horse, this head was carved from an antler by a Cro-Magnon artist some 13,000 years ago. Although only two inches across, it is so lifelike that it has earned the title "whinnying horse," and even its species can be identified—Equus przewalskii.

eventual conquest by man seems in many ways a fantastic achievement.

But something else besides the horse's temperament postponed the first ride: the small size of early domesticated horses. Stock taken willy-nilly from the wild herds that roamed the central and western steppes probably stood no higher than 12 or 13 hands, or just a bit over four feet; this is the average size of the Przewalski horse, the only wild species to survive into modern times. Domesticated horses bred from such stock would have been too small to serve as mounts suited for hunting or war.

Such pony-sized horses, however, proved vastly superior to onagers as pullers of chariots, and in this role the horse became common in the Near East during the Second Millennium B.C. Before that time the onager-drawn chariot had been employed in the Near East both for warfare and for transport. Four- and two-wheeled vehicles in Mesopotamia, according to depictions that go back to 3000 B.C., were limited conveyances indeed.

The cumbersome, difficult-to-steer, four-wheeled chariot—with its small, heavy, solid wooden wheels that rotated with the axle—was eventually displaced by the more flexible two-wheeler. This type, in its simplest form, was a kind of straddle car. It, too, had solid wheels but they rotated independently of the axle. Its body was little more than a plank fixed as a continuation of the draft pole to which onagers were hitched. Atop this plank, just in front of the axle, was a small platform. Here the driver would stand astride the center plank, using reins and a nose ring to direct a pair of yoked onagers.

In time improvements were made in the basic design. Some chariots could be pulled by two or even four onagers, and enough room was provided for a driver and a warrior, both of whom stood in a light body of wickerwork and were guarded by a high dashboard. Such chariots, although slow and cumbrous even when drawn by a team of four onagers, may have been used by the Mesopotamian kings of Agade and Ur to maintain communications within their sprawling domains.

Eventually horses had replaced the onagers as chariot animals. Not only were the horses stronger, but they were swifter. With the introduction of the lighter, spoked wheel around 1700 B.C., the chariot was no longer a ponderous, rumbling vehicle but was well on its way to becoming a swift-moving platform for a fighting man. Just where the spoked wheel originated no one knows. It may have been a Mesopotamian or Caucasian invention. In the Caucasus both ample timber and centuries of familiarity with wheeled vehicles probably stimulated experiments aimed at continuing improvements.

This progress in chariot design was accompanied by another great technological advance—the addition to the horse's noseband of bits, made of leather, rope and eventually metal, with cheekpieces to which reins were attached. The driver now had better control of the horse, and as the chariot became an instrument of communication as well as war, conquerors like the Hittites, Assyrians and Egyptians could use it to build bigger, more cohesive empires.

As the need for chariots grew, so did the need for larger, powerful horses to pull them, and men, as they domesticated the animals, began to increase the horses' size through breeding. In the wild, horses had to rely on forage alone for sustenance; even after being domesticated they were at first left to fend for themselves, and often starved during the long winter months on the steppes. And those that survived were too skinny and weak to be of much use in spring. So man learned to supply some of the animals with grains in winter as well as with some kind of shelter. The results must soon have become apparent. Not only did the horses look better—their coats, for example, turned sleek and shiny—but they also grew larger. Over a period of several generations, well-cared-for mounts stood inches taller than those that had been left to forage for themselves the year round. In contrast, domestic horses that wandered off returned to a smaller average size in the course of just a few generations.

Thus men molded the horse, and the day gradually approached when they would regularly ride it. The earliest-known proof that some had done so, discovered in an Egyptian tomb dated at 1350 B.C., is a wooden figure of a horse ridden by a groom. Further, Egyptian battle scenes carved on monuments that were completed around 1300 B.C. include occasional riders—some of them apparently dispatch bearers, others defeated enemies escaping the carnage on loose chariot horses. Excavations in Greece have turned up a crude clay figurine of a horse and rider that dates back to about the same period.

The interesting thing about all these finds is that they show poor riding technique: men using the so-called donkey seat (page 62)—that is, sitting well back toward the horse's rump. (The origin of the term lies in the fact that when one rides a donkey, it is much more comfortable to straddle the broad rump than the sharp ridge of the animal's backbone.) Moreover, the rump seat on an animal of small size gave the rider of old an extra bit of height that kept his feet from dragging on the ground.

Large-eyed Przewalski horses like these once roamed the steppes by the tens of thousands; by mid-20th Century fewer than 300 survived, though their numbers were rising as the result of breeding programs in both Europe and America.

After the 14th Century B.C., depictions of riding became increasingly widespread in the Near East as well as in Greece, but still showed the horses being ridden awkwardly. For example, Assyrian cavalrymen of the Ninth Century B.C. required aides to ride beside them and manage their mounts so that they would be free to use their weapons (page 62).

More than a century passed before the Assyrians, learning from more skilled horsemen, like the Scythians, began to feel at home on horseback. But how painful the learning process must have been: the contoured saddle as it is known today did not come into existence until the Fourth Century A.D., and stirrups not until the Sixth Century A.D. The first horsemen simply threw cloths over their mounts to cushion the ride, and their legs dangled free.

But where and when did the first true ride take place? How did the horseman's skills evolve? Inevitably the answers are hedged and shadowy. The time can be no more securely pinned down than to say the ride occurred at some undetermined date after about 3500 B.C., when the people of the Ukraine began to keep horses. As for the region where it occurred, some scholars focus on the steppes of south Russia or Central Asia. Others single out the steppe just south of the Caucasus Mountains in northern Iran. The evidence is scant in all three regions. The first man to ride with equipment durable enough to survive the ravages of centuries and to be dug up intact certainly was not the first man ever to mount a horse. The very first rider, using primitive equipment consisting perhaps of no more than reins attached to a noseband, would have left traces only slightly more lasting than the hoofprints of his horse.

An Ancient Guide to Horsemanship

One of the earliest treatises on horsemanship, written in the Fourth Century B.C., is a comprehensive and unique how-to guide for riders. Its author, the Athenian Xenophon, was a commander in the Greek army and a master of cavalry tactics. In an appendix to an essay he wrote on the duties of a cavalry officer, he turned his attention to the horse itself. The result is a remarkable set of step-by-step instructions on every aspect of horsemanship. Excerpts from this ancient handbook—as valid today as when it was written—appear below.

Gentling the Colt

Care must be taken that when the young horse is sent to the breaker he is gentle, used to being handled and friendly. This result is best obtained if the colt associates hunger and thirst and the attacks of insects with solitude, and eating and drinking and freedom from things that hurt him with men.

And one should touch those parts where a horse particularly enjoys being stroked, that is the most hairy parts and those which the horse is least able to protect himself if anything troubles him. The groom should lead the young horse through crowds and make him approach sights and sounds of all sorts. And whenever any of them frightens him he must be taught, not by rough treatment but by coaxing, that there is no danger.

Care and Grooming

When grooming the horse, one should begin with the head and mane. For if the upper parts are dirty it is useless to clean those below. On the rest of the body all the grooming instruments may be employed. The hair should be lifted, and the dirt wiped off in the direction of the lie of the coat. But the hair along the spine must not be touched with any tool but rubbed with the hands and smoothed the way it lies by nature. For this will do least injury to the part of the horse on which the rider sits.

Water must be used to wash the head. For it is bony, and cleaning it with iron or wood would hurt the horse. And the forelock should be wetted. For when the hair of the forelock is long it does not obstruct the horse's vision but drives off noxious insects from the eyes.

The mane ought to be washed, since the hair must grow long to give the rider as much as possible to hold on to. We do not recommend washing the legs. For it does no good, and daily wetting injures the hooves. Excessive grooming under the belly should be reduced to a minimum. For it causes the greatest annoyance to the horse.

Calming a Spirited Mount

You must understand first of all that spirit is to a horse what anger is to a man. And just as one would be least likely to anger a man if one neither said nor did anything to displease him, so a spirited horse is least likely to be enraged by someone who does not excite him. When you are mounted you must calm him for a longer time than an average horse, and in making him advance use the aids as gently as possible. And then you must begin at the slowest pace and gradually proceed to a faster, in such a way that the horse may as far as possible not notice his increased speed. But if anyone expects, by riding fast and far, to tire the horse out and in that way make him gentle, his opinion is contrary to reality. For in such circumstances the spirited horse tries his hardest to bolt and in his anger, like a proud-hearted man, often inflicts fatal injuries both on himself and his rider.

Winning a Horse's Favor

If you ever wish to treat a good war horse so as to make him more magnificent and spectacular to ride, you must avoid pulling at his mouth with the bit and spurring and whipping him, by which behavior most people think they make their horses brilliant. For these people obtain a result quite contrary to their intentions. For by pulling the mouths up in the air they blind their horses instead of letting them see where they are going, and by spurring and whipping they bewilder the animals so that they are confused to the point of danger. But if you teach a horse to go on a slack rein with his neck raised high, flexing at the back of the head, in this way you cause him to act just as he does of his own accord when pleased and enjoying himself.

And it can be proved that he does enjoy these actions. For when he wants to display himself in front of other horses, especially in front of mares, he lifts his neck up high and flexes his poll haughtily and picks up his legs freely and keeps his tail up. And so when you bring a horse to carry himself in the manner in which he himself displays himself when he is showing off as much as he can, you prove that he is enjoying his work and is magnificent, proud and spectacular.

The circumstances can of course only be imagined. But no writer has more richly conjured up what may have occurred than the Danish author Johannes V. Jensen (1873-1950). The son of a veterinary surgeon, he knew horses intimately, and as author of a cycle of novels about the evolution of man, he was awarded the 1944 Nobel Prize for literature.

In one of those books, *The Glacier,* Jensen envisions a family living in a settlement on the fringe of the steppe. The family keeps horses both for meat and for pulling sledges and carts. The animals are pastured in a large paddock hemmed in on three sides by water and, on the fourth, by a ditch. Sons of the family catch and halter the horses to lead them back to the settlement for hitching. And in the course of their chores, they attempt riding—with, at first, violent results, just as would happen today with an unbroken horse:

"It was not to be thought of that the horse would tolerate a man on his inviolable back. The inherited experience of generations made the horse blindly resist the slightest advances of that kind."

Every time one of the boys tried to maintain a hold on the animal's back, "you could see the offended horse spring straight up into the air with all four feet to send him to the stars, and if he actually kept his seat then a vertical rear with the hindquarters and the next instant up with the forelegs the same way, and if this pitching didn't make him seasick, then a wild jump to one side and up with the back in an arch that nobody could hang on to: but if he stuck on all the same . . . why then there was nothing for it but (the horse must) roll on the ground, or a heap of stones for choice, with all four legs in the air to get rid of the vermin; or it might be necessary to rush at full gallop for a tree with a low bough that would shake him off."

One of the sons, named Wolf, eventually finds the way to tap what Jensen romantically calls the "secret sympathy" between horse and man, an "obscure memory" dating far back to a time when the ancestors of both existed side by side in the wild. The youth pampers a stallion born in captivity; from its birth, he pets and befriends it. He learns to approach it always with enormous calm, with never a sudden, unexpected movement. He feeds it morsels and rubs it endlessly, sweet-talking all the time, slowly accustoming the stallion to his presence, to the touch of his hand. As for the horse:

"Its innate shyness lay so deep in its blood that it was ready to start off all the time as though possessed by a thousand promptings of light, quivering in every joint and with wide, fleeting eyes; its ear, twitching nervously, lay back flat while its teeth showed in an ugly grin; its nostrils stretched so that the daylight gleamed through the rosy cartilage between them; it wanted to be patted and yet did not want it, swung its flank forward and drew back ticklishly, as though it was fire it felt and not a human hand; its mood shifted like a breeze on the water; only after a long, long time of tireless overtures would it accept the relationship, but really *tame* it never was."

First by leaning against its flank and then by draping his arms across its back, the boy named Wolf gradually accustoms the horse to his weight. Then, at last the moment comes when he raises himself onto the back and is astride—and the horse lets him be. It begins to walk, but before long the pair are galloping around the paddock, then out onto the open expanse

Finery for Well-bred Steeds

From tombs in Siberia's Altai Mountains has come vivid proof of how much importance the horsemen attached to their mounts, which even accompanied them to the grave. Among the remains of these horses were bones of especially tall and well-kept geldings, with saddles, bridles and headdresses still in place, the basis for the artist's rendering below. No doubt feeding the horses grain and sheltering them during winter helped their appearance, but early gelding, which extends the period of growth of the long bones and the cervical vertebrae, enhanced it even more, giving the mounts taller bodies and longer, slimmer necks.

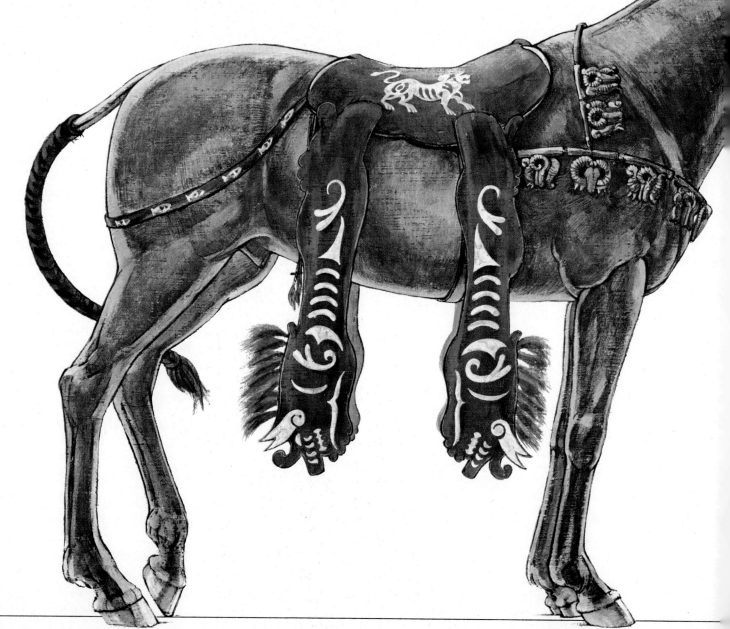

Stuffed with deer hair, this primitive saddle cushioned the thighs of the rider and softened his ride. Made of felt, it is appliquéd with multicolored figures of a griffin seizing a mountain goat. The pendants are edged in horsehair and fur, dyed red and blue respectively.

Adorned in all its earthly finery, a beautiful mount stands ready for sacrifice and burial near its master at Pazyryk. The horse's face mask has perforated ear sheaths, and terminates in a pair of stylized antlers. Cutouts of felt, leather and foil decorate the saddlecloth and its pendants, and red horsehair tops the stiff mane cover.

of steppe: "The first horseman, with a scrap of wolf's skin tied about his middle and his fiery hair flying about his ears. . . . Wolf moulded in one with the wild horse, still half-striped like a zebra, its shoulders marked with lightning, and with the thunderbolt under each of its heart-shaped hoofs!"

It could well have happened as Jensen imagined. But however the first ride really came about, the ensuing alliance between man and horse increased the rider's capacities enormously. The world about him was suddenly diminished, the horizon was at once more extended in space, yet also brought closer. The mounted man had become larger than life, and he irresistibly looked down on his earth-bound contemporaries with condescension. The charioteer had only indirectly and incompletely profited by the powers of the horse; the man astride now shared these powers directly and fully, and for the first time he knew the excitement of performance beyond his own physical limitations.

If the horse radically increased the range of man, its effect on his mind was at least as great. His new power enlarged his vision and heightened his sense of worth. It also inflamed his vanity, engendering arrogance of the kind that is meant even today when someone is spoken of as being "on his high horse," or when the word "pedestrian" is used with overtones of contempt, or when a powerful leader is described as "the man on horseback." A story told by the Greek philosopher Diogenes Laertius, writing in the Third Century A.D., had it that Plato, some 500 years earlier, had once mounted a horse at the insistence of friends, but immediately dismounted lest he be overcome with "horse pride."

Abundant proof that man felt exalted by the horse appears in his own exaltation of the horse. Images of the creature came to be carved on the walls of temples, rendered in statue form, painted, stamped on coins and celebrated in poetry and romance. The ancient Hebrew word for horse, abbir, also meant "strong" and "valiant." The chieftains of the Scythians, as well as those of other tribes of nomadic horsemen who evolved on the steppes, even carried their mounts with them to the grave.

Herodotus says that the Scythians also considered the horse a suitable sacrifice to their gods, and some peoples of antiquity, going a step farther, elevated the creature to their pantheon. In the ancient religious myths of India, for example, the gods of the sun, the moon and lightning were represented as horses. Many of the gods and heroes of classical civilizations would have had difficulty functioning without their steeds: Mars, the Roman god of war, often was portrayed on horseback, and without the assistance of his winged horse, Pegasus, the semidivine Bellerophon of Greek mythology might never have conquered the Amazons.

Down into Christian times the horse remained an object of religious awe or veneration. In the New Testament, St. John depicted the four figures of the Apocalypse—famine, war, plague and death—as horsemen. And ridden by such saints as St. George and St. Martin, the horse in the Middle Ages was the emblem of courage and generosity.

Man sometimes even attributed occult powers to the beast. Tacitus, the Roman historian, describes how Germanic tribesmen kept pure white horses "in their sacred groves, untouched and free from any sort of mortal labor" to be consulted by kings and other

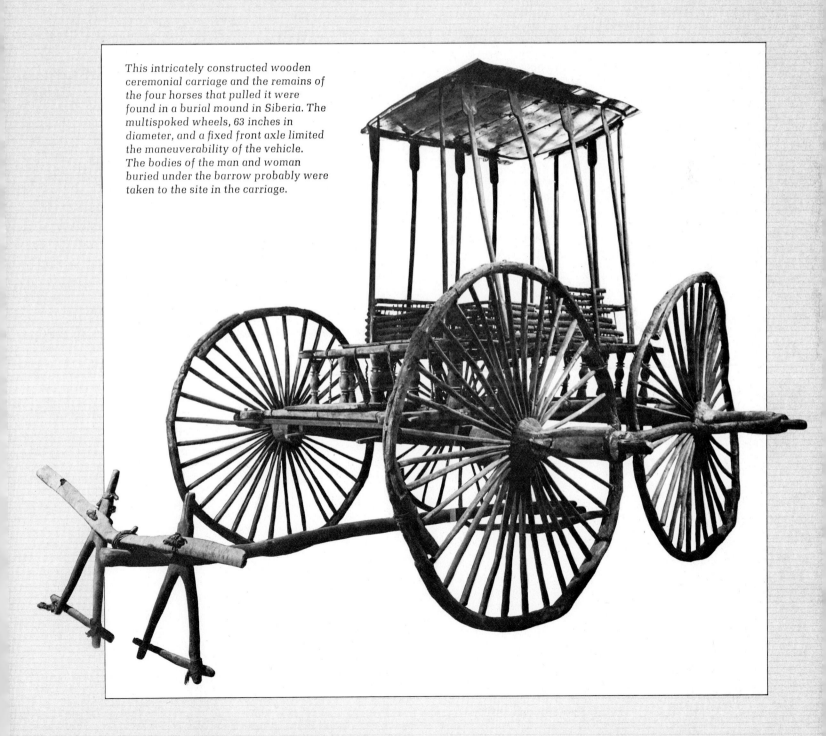

This intricately constructed wooden ceremonial carriage and the remains of the four horses that pulled it were found in a burial mound in Siberia. The multispoked wheels, 63 inches in diameter, and a fixed front axle limited the maneuverability of the vehicle. The bodies of the man and woman buried under the barrow probably were taken to the site in the carriage.

dignitaries who took guidance and prophecy from their whinnyings and neighings. The horse may even have played a key role in determining the course of ancient history: legend says that Darius the Great became king of Persia after his rivals for the throne agreed to yield to the one whose horse first neighed on an appointed morning.

Mystical awe of the horse persisted until relatively recently, particularly among primitive peoples. Even in the early 20th Century when a boy was born to the Patagonian Indians of southern South America, he was placed inside the freshly opened stomach of a mare or colt. The ceremony was calculated to imbue the infant with the attributes of a centaur. And down to today a certain magical view of the horse lingers in the widespread view of the horseshoe as a symbol of good luck.

While the spread of horseback riding profoundly affected the mind and mobility of man and clearly altered patterns of life in nearly all parts of the earth, in most places the change took place gradually. But on the Eurasian steppes, where riding began, it engendered with astonishing suddenness a whole new way of existence among tribes long accustomed to village life based on a simple, changeless pattern of agriculture and stock raising.

Hard, archeological evidence of this time-honored way of life is fairly plentiful across the steppes. What tantalizes scholars is the lack of specific evidence surrounding the events that so swiftly transformed that sedentary, relatively peaceful society into one of aggressive, nomadic horsemen who galloped through much of the ancient world. The only clues to that abrupt transition were the imprints of those "heart-shaped hoofs," but they were as transitory as the clouds of dust they kicked up behind them.

The Miraculous Partnership between Man and Mount

Long before man learned to seat himself firmly and confidently astride a horse's back, the animal had served him in other ways: first as a wild creature hunted for its meat and hide, then—after it had been tamed—as a source of milk and eventually as fast motive power for his chariots. When man finally became a rider, he was still far from being an accomplished equestrian. Only after he had developed the skills and equipment that gave him full control over his spirited, powerful steed did he feel completely at ease on the horse, able to run down the fleetest game or to spread terror and carnage as he galloped into battle against unmounted foes.

Cheekpieces, like this Eighth Century B.C. bronze one from northern Iran, were attached to the bit to hold it in the horse's mouth.

Charioteers—Precursors of Mounted Warriors

As one man drives a two-wheeled chariot, another takes aim with his bow in this impression from an inch-long, 3,500-year-old gold seal found in a Mycenaean grave. The scene, a deer hunt, is the earliest-known Greek depiction of a chariot drawn by a horse.

From his fast-moving chariot, behind a team of horses with wrapped tails, the Assyrian king Ashurnasirpal hunts lions, the lordly pastime of ancient monarchs. The light, spoke-wheeled chariot shown on a Ninth Century B.C. relief from his palace at Nimrud represents a marked improvement over earlier Mesopotamian chariots, which had solid wheels and were hitched not to horses but to less powerful onagers.

From Awkward Equestrian to Master Rider

Perched precariously far back toward his horse's rump, a position more suitable for sitting on a donkey, this bareback rider from an Egyptian battle scene of about 1350 B.C. is obviously not a skilled horseman. The long reins suggest that he has fled from the conflict on an escaped chariot horse.

On an Assyrian bronze relief of around 850 B.C., mounted archers are still riding badly, retaining the Egyptian "donkey seat" (see above). So unsteady are the Assyrians on their horses that they are being led by aides who hold onto the reins while the warriors use their bows.

No longer clumsy or apprehensive on horseback, Assyrian hunters of the Seventh Century B.C., even though they lack the support of stirrups, control their mounts easily and with confidence. As depicted on this relief from Nineveh, they ride well forward, gripping their steeds securely with knees and calves, displaying the good horsemanship that they may have learned from the Scythians, Assyria's sometime ally in war.

A New and Deadly Expertise

With the art of riding mastered, the mounted warrior could concentrate less on staying astride his horse and more on the development of such skills as the so-called Parthian shot being delivered here by a proud Scythian. One of four figures encircling the top of an 18-inch-high, late Sixth Century bronze vessel found in southern Italy (right), he apparently guides his horse by knee pressure, leaving both hands free to launch an arrow over his animal's rump—a battle tactic that was characteristic of the Scythians.

The Role of the Horse in Legend and Myth

On a Fifth Century B.C. Attic vase, a mounted Amazonian warrior spears a fallen foe. The Greeks' account of these legendary horsewomen may have been partly inspired by the Sarmatian women, who lived to the east of the Scythians and who rode herd with their men and galloped beside them into battle.

The swiftness, stamina and grace of the horse so captured the imagination of man that he sometimes merged with the animal in his mythology. This 14-inch-high Ninth Century B.C. centaur is from the Greek island of Euboea.

Poised for flight, a winged horse adorns a two-inch-high gold plaque found in a Fourth Century B.C. Scythian grave in the Crimea, which was once under strong Greek influence. The horse represents the mythical Greek steed Pegasus.

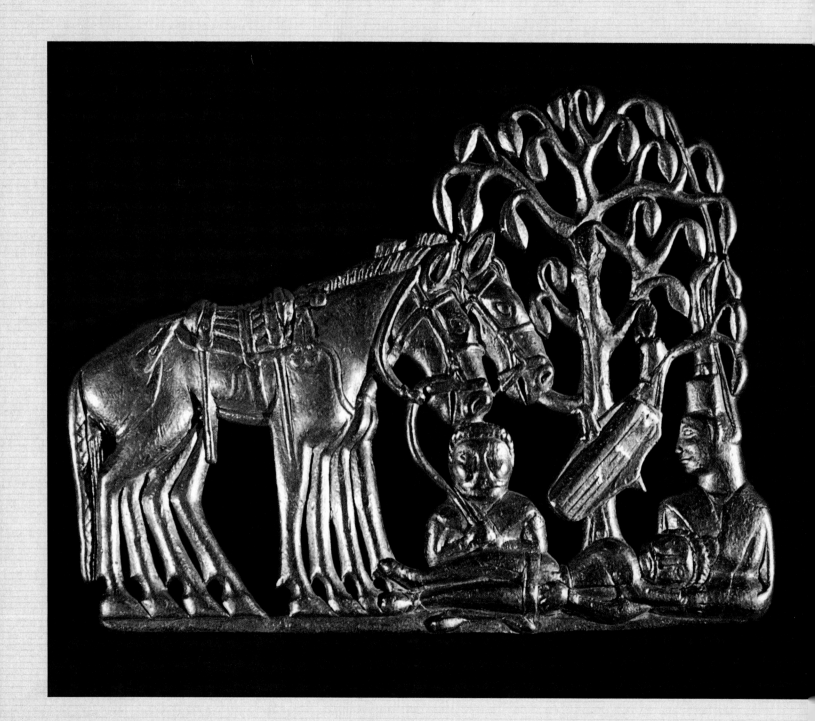

Horseback riding, whenever and wherever it originated, had profound and enduring effects upon the inhabitants of the steppes, working a transformation so revolutionary that the essential story of these vigorous people can be divided into two periods: before and after the first horsemen. The sudden emergence of riders among scattered seminomadic tribes sometime around 900 B.C. engendered an utterly new kind of social organization, supremely mobile and far-flung, which was to outlast every contemporaneous civilization. Indeed, this "peculiar form of society," as one scholar has described it, flourished to the beginnings of the modern industrial era, a span of 2,700 years. And in some undeveloped parts of Asia, remnants of it exist even today.

The immense region in which this dynamic society rose is an awesome swath of almost horizonless earth that lies like a ragged mantle across the shoulders of two continents. Most of it consists of grassy plains, broken only by wooded river valleys. In the west these plains begin at the Carpathians on the eastern border of Hungary and spill down across part of Rumania to the Danube and the coast of the Black Sea. Curving northward around the Black and Azov seas, they traverse the area of south Russia that became the domain of the Scythians. From there they dip southward into the Caucasus and spread onward through a channel formed by the northern shore of

In a tranquil mood, two nomad warriors and a lady wearing a tall headdress repose under a leafy tree on whose branch is hanging a bow-and-arrow case. The hand-held tether and bridled horses suggest that the party will soon move on. This six-inch-long ornament, once worn on a belt, formed part of the golden treasure plundered from Siberian graves and presented to Peter the Great in the 18th Century.

the Caspian Sea and the southernmost extension of the Urals—the mountain wall that marks the end of Europe and the beginning of Asia.

In Asia the grasslands skirt the Aral Sea and roll on eastward across Siberia, above the largely desert steppe of the regions of Kazakhstan and Zungaria, north of the Tien Shan range of western China. Now, some 2,500 miles from their western edge in Europe, the grasslands meet their first great obstacle, the Altai ranges, forming the border between western Mongolia and Siberia. Beyond the Altai—in a plateau region spotted with arid areas—the grasslands flow around another barrier, the Gobi Desert. Beyond the Gobi, they curve gradually northward until they finally peter out at the foothills of the Khingan Mountains fringing western Manchuria.

Here on the steppes—in this sea of grass—the first horsemen would come to be. But for at least 2,000 years before their emergence as full-fledged riders, their ancestors would be restricted in movement, limited to certain areas. Just when and how these people arrived in the grasslands no one knows. Many scholars, understanding full well the controversy surrounding the subject, conjecture that they sprang from the same stock as the Indo-European-speaking groups who spread out from some undetermined homeland in a series of far-reaching migrations. Some moved into the Balkan Peninsula and became the ancient Greeks. Others pushed into the civilized lands of western Asia to become the forefathers of the Medes and Persians. Still other Indo-European-speaking migrants pressed as far as India.

Those whose descendants became the first horsemen remained north of the Caucasus and eventually settled down on the steppes, mainly in the fertile wooded valleys of the great rivers that threaded the plains. In Russia they lived along the lower Dnieper, Don and Volga. Beyond the Urals in Siberia they inhabited the banks of the Irtysh and the Ob, and some dwelled as far east as the valley of the Yenisei, north of the Altai Mountains.

By about 1500 B.C. the settlers of the steppes were pursuing a mixed economy based largely on stockbreeding. They raised large numbers of sheep for meat and wool, and in some regions kept pigs as well. They also maintained herds of cattle for food and hides, and used the strongest of the animals to pull their two-wheeled carts and four-wheeled wagons. At this time they apparently regarded their horses only as beasts to milk and slaughter—though they may well have been impressed by their grace and speed. In addition to livestock, the settlers raised wheat, barley and millet. They also hunted and fished, probably more from choice than necessity, and occasionally did some trading with foreigners to obtain metal tools and ornaments.

No matter how far apart their settlements, the various steppe tribes seem to have had many features in common—perhaps a consequence of living in so broad and sweeping an environment, capped by an enormous dome of sky. From the archeological evidence their villages had quite similar layouts. Most stood on the higher, well-drained land of the river valleys and consisted of wood and wattle houses that numbered from 10 to 20. These dwellings and their enclosures, or sheds, for livestock typically stood arranged in rows, often along both sides of a "street." Built directly on the ground or with foundations sunk a couple of feet into the earth, the houses varied in shape: some were square, others rectangular or

A Chronology of the First Horsemen

3200 B.C.
Horse domesticated on south Russian steppe.

1700 B.C.
Horse-drawn chariot introduced in Near East.

1500 B.C.
Seminomadic stockbreeding tribes inhabit steppes.

c. 900 B.C.
Spread of mounted nomadism.

707 B.C.
Cimmerians, earliest-known mounted nomads, defeat kingdom of Urartu in Near East.

c. 700 B.C.
Scythian presence in Near East recorded in Assyrian texts.

674 B.C.
Scythian king marries daughter of Esarhaddon, ruler of the Assyrian Empire.

612 B.C.
Medes, with Scythians, capture Nineveh and destroy Assyrian Empire.

c. 600 B.C.
Medes drive Scythians north of the Caucasus.

514 B.C.
Scythians, now dominant in south Russia, repel Persian invasion under Darius the Great.

c. 450 B.C.
Herodotus visits Greek trading colony of Olbia to gather information on Scythians.

c. 350 B.C.
Sarmatians begin to enter Scythian territory. Little Scythia founded in Rumania.

339 B.C.
Scythians, under King Ateas, defeated in battle in Rumania by Philip of Macedon.

331 B.C.
Scythians annihilate an army of Alexander the Great in Black Sea region.

214 B.C.
Chinese complete Great Wall as defense against Hsiung-nu.

c. 200 B.C.
Scythians withdraw to Crimea, establish capital at Neapolis and impose heavy tribute on Greek colonies.

110-106 B.C.
Scythians in Crimea defeated by Pontic king Mithradates the Great. Black Sea area is gradually drawn into Rome's sphere of influence.

round; some were tiny, others as large as 30 by 50 feet. A thick layer of reeds or branches, covered with grass or earth, served as roofing, and soil or stones with planks constituted flooring. Each house had a central stone hearth; some of the larger, later dwellings had the luxury of two fireplaces.

Confronted by the trackless expanses of the steppes, the settlers had good reason to stick close to the riverbanks. The rivers themselves must have served as highways along which or on which they could travel both winter and summer, and the valleys, being lower than the surrounding landscape, must have offered a degree of protection from the wind. The rich soil of the banks would have encouraged good crops, and the rivers themselves provided an unfailing supply of water. Near the delta of the Amu Darya on the Aral Sea, Soviet archeologists have discovered traces of irrigation ditches used to carry water to the fields.

Life in such settlements was limited by certain realities. The settlers raised only as many animals as they could conveniently keep track of. They could tend sheep on foot, but without riding horses to help them manage their herds on a fenceless range, they were unable to push far out onto the open steppes. Some of them, however, did migrate seasonally within limited areas, as the discovery of a few temporary campsites in Siberia shows.

Existence could not have been easy on the steppes. And yet these people—whose names disappeared centuries ago and who in many places left traces hardly more tangible than shadows—seem to have flourished. Moreover, they had time for such pursuits as the fashioning of personal ornaments and the decorating of pottery.

Partly through the differences in ceramic bowls and pots, archeologists have identified the various tribes and tracked their rises and falls. For example, early settlers of western Siberia indulged a fancy for pots with flared rims and overall zigzag and triangular designs, while later settlers in the same area preferred pots with unflared rims and designs limited to the necks.

Archeologists are also able to sort out the various steppe tribes through differences in their burial customs (pages 72-73). In south Russia, for example, early settlers dug square or rectangular shafts for their dead, often lining such graves with timber, and sprinkling the bodies with red ocher—perhaps to restore the ruddy coloration of life. Later settlers in the same region added lateral niches to shaft graves; because of this habit, they are referred to today as the Catacomb Grave people. Settlers east of the Black Sea constructed chambers like huts inside their graves, complete with paved stone floors and wooden roofs; they are known as the Timber Grave people. Still others, representing a confused diversity of tribes in western Siberia, walled their graves with large rocks or tree trunks and marked them with slabs or circles of stones; they are referred to as the Andronovo people, after the name of an excavation site on the Yenisei River.

In fact, the way of death among the early steppe dwellers receives such detailed attention in archeological reports that it is sometimes easy to forget that these people also *lived,* that they tasted the salt of their own sweat, felt the warmth of the sun on their skin or the coolness of an approaching storm as the sky darkened and then exploded with the sudden fury of thunder and lightning.

Two Millennia of Burial Mounds

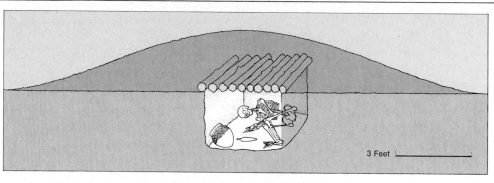

Pit graves, hewn out of the soil, roofed with a layer of logs and topped by small mounds of earth, first came into use around the Third Millennium B.C. The dead were interred with a few possessions: a clay pot, a stone tool or two and copper trinkets.

As early as 3000 B.C., long before the emergence of the first horsemen, tribesmen on the grasslands and in the river valleys of eastern Europe, Central Asia and southern Siberia buried their dead in underground chambers beneath mounds of earth and stones. From aboveground the hummock-like grave markers vary only in size, but below them lie four distinct types of tombs. Archeologists refer to them as pit, cist, catacomb and timber graves, according to their shapes and constructions. The contents of the tombs have provided most of what we know of the farmers and stockbreeders who first inhabited the steppes.

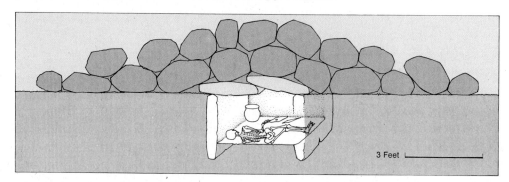

Walled with stone slabs and mounded over by rocks, cist graves were used as early as 2500 B.C., mainly in the Caucasus. Tools of metal, usually bronze, and pottery vessels accompanied the dead. A thousand years later, similar tombs were built in southern Siberia.

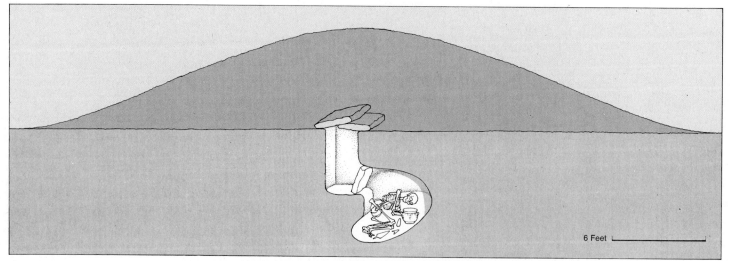

Catacomb graves—so called for their complex stepped-down, L-shaped conformation—developed around 1500 B.C., to the northeast of the Black Sea. The dead, concealed behind stone slab barricades, were buried with their possessions and the bones of domesticated animals.

Elaborate timber graves, like the one sketched at right and shown as reconstructed in a model (below) in Moscow, became common in the region north of the Black Sea around the middle of the Second Millennium B.C., and were in use for over 1,000 years. The burial chamber was topped with a timbered hut, then covered with a mound in which were buried not only pots, weapons and finery but also sheep, cattle and, on occasion, horses.

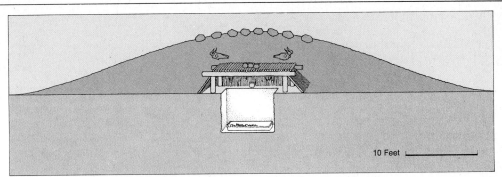

10 Feet

For all the many steppe tribes, as for man in the Bible, there was a time for all things in the changeless ritual of chores, duties and pleasures. On any day and in any village, in the gray stirrings of dawn, the children gathered dried cattle dung for the fires and hauled up the morning water from the river. On any day it was necessary to milk the cows, ewes and mares in the livestock enclosures and to watch herds let out to pasture. In each house, grain had to be ground and bread baked on the hearths. And mare's milk fermenting in a leather sack had to be monotonously churned—perhaps by a child watching an eagle soar to a speck and finally vanish altogether in the endless sky of summer.

At night, in good weather, the villagers sat outside around a fire and sang or listened to the stories of one of their bards, while beyond the ring of firelight a prowling wildcat or wolf set the livestock to a nervous pattering of hoofs. The bard would tell of the great hunts and struggles of the past, of how the gods had withdrawn their favors or showered down blessings. And then, as the fires died, the tribesmen would retire to the comfort of their dwellings, there to sleep through the long, star-studded night.

In addition to daily activities, there were seasonal tasks: sheep to be shorn of their thick winter wool in springtime, hides to be cured for clothing, and felt to be made into yurt coverings and boots. And in all seasons the men probably taught the boys how to use the bow. In those early days the bow was still primarily a hunter's tool. Out of the tribesmen's proficiency with the bow would one day come the horsemen's deadly use of it against their foes.

So it went, century after century, across the whole immense span of the steppes. Cultural interactions between tribes no doubt went on, and changes occurred. But invariably the changes—or at least those that archeology has revealed—seem to have been in the material sphere, as the settlers built more and larger houses to accommodate the growing population, used more metals for tools and ornaments, and placed more elaborate offerings in the graves of their important dead. On the whole, however, the routine of life continued much as it always had—and apparently largely in peace.

Then suddenly, in or about the Ninth Century B.C., some overpowering new ferment began to sweep through this straggle of tribes. Something dislocated them, transformed them. Something came and moved so swiftly that archeology has not been able to detect the transition, only the results.

Peoples who had been previously distinct became mingled. Groups that once had been restricted to the river valleys started moving far out onto the steppes. Battle-axes, spearheads, arrowheads grew in number. Some cultures vanished abruptly. Far away to the east, around the Yenisei River in Siberia, similar signs of rapid social change appeared.

What had happened? The age of the horseman —the long and turbulent age of the Scythian, the Sarmatian, the Hun and the Mongol—had dawned. The art of horseback riding spread like some marvelous epidemic among the tribes of the Eurasian steppes. It transformed tribal life, collapsing old structures and creating new. Some of its effects were immediate, others followed quickly. The horse at once extended the tribesman's range and capacity as a hunter, giving him for the first time an advantage over such big, swift quarries as elk and bison. More important, he had precisely what he required to control larger herds of cattle. He also had what was needed to build and control ever greater numbers of horses. Mounted, he could methodically wrangle the best specimens out of the small, unmanageable clusters of wild horses on the steppes, running them down as foals and breeding them at maturity to his bigger and more tractable domestic stock.

Out of this widening of horizons came other changes. Keeping bigger herds demanded more and better grazing lands. No longer limited in their range, as had been their forebears, the herdsmen now pushed out over greater distances for longer periods. As they did so, their ties to the settled communities of their farmer kinfolk weakened. And inevitably, as they broke out of the old familiar precincts, their contact with other herdsmen increased—and a true society of horsemen came into being. The idea of riding rippled in ever-expanding rings across the steppes, not only separating herdsmen from farmers but also creating new groups whose sole business was raising and maintaining livestock.

As the demand for pasturage grew, the tribes began to compete, and inevitably conflicts must have arisen between claimants to the same range. In a time when might was unarguably right, the most powerful herdsmen could doubtless control the best pastures. Clearly, they could seize their competitors' stock as well. Vanquished tribes must soon have learned by bitter experience that they could protect their interests only by joining forces against the mighty intruder. In some such way alliances and federations of tribes gradually came into being, until they swelled into what would be called hordes—and the riders began to plunge into contact with peoples living on the peripheries of the steppes.

Within the steppes, the earlier communal relationship of the herdsman and the farmer had been irrevocably altered. Even the earliest mounted nomads, inflated by the heightened sense of power that riding gave to the individual, could not fail to see that the pedestrian farmer was at their mercy. In the face of mounted fighters, the peasants could choose only to scatter, to die—or to cooperate in a relationship by which they supplied grain and other commodities to the riders. No doubt most chose to cooperate. By the time the horsemen entered history, the settled farmers had long been accustomed to meeting their demands. As Herodotus noted, the Royal Scythians looked upon all the ancillary tribes of their south Russian domain as slaves.

The horseman was a new breed of man. He was not a mere rider and keeper of horses, nor did he simply exploit the horse: he merged with his mount in a remarkably thorough way. He reshaped his entire mode of life around the capabilities of the horse. He stripped himself of all identification with a permanent home and became a full-fledged nomad who, with his herds, followed the seasonal grasses with scant regard for distance. His dwelling had become a collapsible tent, his hearth could be anywhere.

Here was total adjustment to the horse as the pivotal fact of life. Without such an adjustment there could not have been the rapid burgeoning of a society as complex, as substantially self-sufficient and as mobile as that of the horsemen of the steppes.

How could such a society have come into being so quickly? The answer lies not in archeology, but in analogy—in the convincing similarity of the swift and revolutionary transformation of the North Amer-

Village Life on a River Terrace

A long time before the people of the steppes took to riding horseback, they found ideal places for village settlements, where the grassy plains sloped into the wooded river valleys of Central Asia and south Russia. In the protective lee of the embankments, on terraces that descended in tiers from the surrounding windy terrain, they built thatch-roofed dwellings, which nestled into the earth's natural contours. A typical village, as it appeared around 1000 B.C., is re-created in this drawing, based on evidence accumulated from excavations near the Volga and Don rivers.

Remarkably self-sufficient, each of the eight- or 10-family settlements supported itself comfortably with an economy based on both stockbreeding and agriculture, supplemented by hunting, fishing and foraging. Natural vegetation sustained small herds of cattle, sheep and horses. In garden patches, amid freestanding houses, millet and barley were cultivated. The river itself yielded fish and shellfish, and from the surrounding woods came game, nuts and berries.

In this scene villagers work to complete the day's chores toward the end of an autumn afternoon. Animals that have been grazing are driven home for the night (upper left); at the riverbank horses are watered, and nearby a woman fires clay pots in a kiln. Two successful hunters (foreground) return carrying a deer, and in preparation for winter, an oxcart has arrived loaded with fodder. In the far distance (upper right) earthen burial mounds are visible on the steppe.

ican Plains Indians after they acquired the horse.

Since the horse was long extinct on the American continents, the Indians' breeding-stock traces to the 10 stallions and six mares brought to Mexico in 1519 by conquistador Hernán Cortés. Others came in with subsequent explorers who gradually pushed northward and colonized great ranches in northern Mexico and in territory that was to become Texas and New Mexico. It may be that strays from Spanish herds occasionally fell into Indian hands, or that horses got away to breed on their own. The Spaniards, however, strived to maintain a strict monopoly on their horses—as on guns. No large numbers of their mounts fell into Indian hands until 1680.

This was the year that the Pueblo Indians declared war on their Spanish oppressors in New Mexico, killing or expelling the colonists almost to a man. The defeated Spaniards left behind several thousand horses. These beasts, through intertribal trading and raids, became distributed northward, and they produced radical changes in Indian life within as little as four decades. Tribes that hitherto had scratched out a living as primitive farmers and as hunters and fishers of limited mobility were suddenly transformed. Now, for the first time, they began to range into the depths of the bison-rich American prairies that had been all but closed to them earlier as realms too enormous to conquer on foot.

"It may be said," writes Benjamin Capps, summing up what other students of American history have said about the Indian and the horse, "that the horse actually created the nomadic Plains Indian as he was encountered by white Americans in the 19th Century —mounted, mobile and fierce, a proud warrior to whom husbandry was anathema and who reveled in

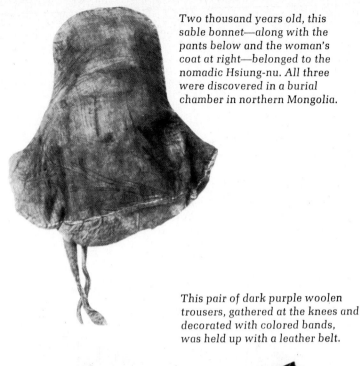

Two thousand years old, this sable bonnet—along with the pants below and the woman's coat at right—belonged to the nomadic Hsiung-nu. All three were discovered in a burial chamber in northern Mongolia.

This pair of dark purple woolen trousers, gathered at the knees and decorated with colored bands, was held up with a leather belt.

A rich silk coat trimmed with sable helped keep out the cold. Although it has faded to a sand color, it was once ruby red.

both the chase after game and the charge against an enemy. From being marginal hunters or farmers plodding at the edge of hunger, many tribes rode the horse into a new life."

This change took only a couple of moments as time is measured on the crawling clock of social evolution. And there is no reason to doubt that the transformation of life on the Eurasian steppes came about just as swiftly. The spread of riding—or, more precisely, the perfection of it—created a society far more complex than that of the isolated groupings of simple farmers. The horse, by augmenting the ambitions and extending the reach of each mounted tribe, bringing them all into ever-quickening communion and conflict, transformed the whole sprawling aggregation of steppe tribes from the Danube River in Europe to the fringes of China into something that had not existed before, a singular and durable social organization for which scholarship has provided no convenient descriptive label.

Perhaps this new order might be called a "nomadization." Certainly it persisted as a distinct alternative to life centered about the city and hence known as civilization. But throughout the long history of this nomadization, civilized folk, overlooking the dynamic qualities and cultures of the nomads, habitually viewed them as barbaric. Often they had good reason to do so. Over and over again the mounted hordes, now one and now another, streamed out of the steppes to intervene violently in the destinies of settled nations to the west, east and south.

Although the Scythians were the first of these hordes whose incursions received the full attention of ancient historians, they were, in a sense, but one

In the first of the scroll's 18 panels, Hsiung-nu horsemen from the Mongolian steppe abduct the white-gowned Lady Wen-chi from the courtyard of her father's elegant house in Shensi province. The marauding nomads were portrayed by the artist as swarthy, in deliberate contrast to the fair-skinned Chinese.

A Chinese Lady and a Nomad Chieftain

Lady Wen-chi, a refined and educated Chinese woman from Shensi, was abducted by a raiding band of horsemen, the Hsiung-nu, in 196 A.D. Carried into Mongolia, she was married to the chieftain and bore him two sons.

After 12 years, she was ransomed by the Chinese. Back home, she recorded her experiences in a poem, whose verses reflect her offended sensibilities in a world of crude men. The scenes at right and on the following pages, illustrating parts of her story, are taken from a 14th Century silk scroll, a copy of the lost original.

branch of a much larger family. Other tribes that throve around the same time shared not only their ferocity on the battlefield, but also many of their ways. As reported by Herodotus, and as confirmed by archeology, the Sarmatians—who long dominated the south Russian steppe east of the Don and who joined the Scythian alliance against the would-be conqueror Darius the Great—had many qualities in common with the Scythians. They, too, were an aggregate, or federation, of tribes, and they even used a language that to ancient observers sounded like Scythian spoken not quite properly.

Only in the status of their women do the Sarmatians seem to have differed from their Scythian neighbors—and in so marked a manner that it is worth digressing to explore the subject briefly. Whereas Scythian women led sheltered lives, the Sarmatian women took part in battle and were as formidable as the menfolk. Their prowess as warriors is attested to by the bows, arrows, swords and other weapons that have turned up in the graves of some of them; one woman's burial site even contained a suit of scale armor. Such archeological evidence tends to bear out ancient Greek accounts that deal with Sarmatian women. Herodotus, for example, reported that the Sarmatians were said to be the offspring of Scythians who had mated with Amazons and that their female descendants "have continued from that day to

After being forced to marry the chieftain, who truly loved her, Lady Wen-chi sits with him in front of a richly decorated, canopied yurt. Musicians serenade them as they wait to be brought their food. Tall felt windscreens, which surround the yurt, protect them from the whirling dust of the steppe.

Desperately unhappy among the coarse Hsiung-nu, the lady wanders off to play her lute. "I have lost my family and my body has been violated," she moans. "Better I had never been born."

the present to observe their ancient (Amazon) customs, frequently hunting on horseback with their husbands, sometimes even unaccompanied; in war taking the field; and wearing the very same dress as the men." Moreover, said Herodotus, "No girl shall wed till she has killed a man in battle."

Hippocrates, the Greek physician who observed the Sarmatians with his specialist's eye, recounted essentially the same information but took particular interest in the operation that turned the women into strong-armed huntresses and fighters.

"They have no right breasts," he noted, "for while they are yet babies their mothers make red-hot a bronze instrument constructed for this very purpose and apply it to the right breast and cauterize it, so that its growth is arrested, and all its strength and bulk are diverted to the right shoulder and right arm." True or not, the story points to the emphasis placed by the ancient riders on physical strength, especially the muscle power needed for hurling spears and shooting arrows great distances.

Only recently have experts begun to comprehend fully the degree to which the communities of steppe tribes were both alike and dissimilar. For example, it was not until the excavation of the famous frozen tombs in the Altai region of Siberia before and after World War II that a range of artifacts convincingly showed that a mounted nomadic society—like the

Lady Wen-chi is at last ransomed for a treasure in gold, and prepares for departure. Wearing a tall hat (center right), she bids her sons farewell; the dark-robed chieftain hides his grief in his hands. Some historians feel that her rescue was part of a larger Chinese plan to buy peace from the Hsiung-nu.

Scythians in "full detail," as one authority puts it, perhaps a bit too enthusiastically—had prospered there at the time of the Scythians' zenith in the Fifth Century B.C. These herdsmen of unknown name who flourished 2,500 miles east of the Scythians' Black Sea domain are called kindred Scythians or eastern Scythians by some scholars; other authorities prefer to be less precise in identifying them, referring to them simply as Altai tribesmen.

In fact, it may be better to be overcautious than too exact in attempting to delineate the many peoples of the nomadization. As time passed, they became a confusion of tribal composites, federations and alliances—as well as a confusion of cultural amalgams that grew still more complex as the mounted way of life spread deep into eastern Asia.

One composite horde that rose to power around the southwestern border of the Gobi Desert during the Third Century B.C. was called the Yueh-Chi —the meat people—by Chinese familiar with their habit of eating raw meat. The tribe seems to have been made up of an Indo-European-speaking people, which suggests a Western origin. How much like the Scythians the Yueh-Chi may have been in their customs is unknown, however, since archeologists have found few of their remains.

Another eastern Asiatic horde that can indeed be said to bear strong resemblances to the Scythians was

the Hsiung-nu; the name means "terrible slaves" in Chinese. This group of herdsmen formed a confederacy that rose to dominance in Mongolia in the Second Century B.C. after it crushed the Yueh-Chi and drove them westward. The racial composition of the Hsiung-nu is obscure. Apparently they were not Mongoloid, for the Chinese against whom they fought considered them foreigners, calling them the northern barbarians and describing them as being hairy, with prominent noses, characteristics more Caucasoid than Mongoloid. The remains of a wall hanging found in the First Century B.C. tomb of a Hsiung-nu chieftain shows men with broad, square, mustached faces of Western type, but this textile could have

been imported from as far away as south Russia.

Parallels between Scythian and Hsiung-nu ways are numerous. Like the Scythians, some of the Hsiung-nu buried their chiefs with many sacrificial victims, and all of them buried revered members of the tribe in grandiose style. Hsiung-nu graves—into which ground water had leaked, helping to preserve the contents by keeping out air—have yielded notable finds that include fine silk clothing of Chinese origin (pages 78-79), elaborate wall hangings and felt carpets richly embroidered with animal designs resembling those favored by the Scythians.

According to ancient Chinese chroniclers, the Hsiung-nu, like the Scythians, practiced polygamy, lived in felt yurts and made drinking cups from their enemies' skulls. Also like the Scythians, and all other mounted nomads of the steppes, they used the bow as their primary weapon.

In their battle tactics, too, the Hsiung-nu resembled the Scythians, retreating when outnumbered and striking back in whirlwind surprise attacks. Just as the Scythians had employed such nerve-racking tactics in holding their own against the best of Darius' troops, so the Hsiung-nu harassed the Chinese, who built the Great Wall in the hope of keeping them in check (page 85).

But even this gigantic barricade of earth, brick and stone, winding more than 2,000 miles across the face of northern China and fortified with watchtowers at regular intervals, discouraged the mounted nomads hardly at all. As the Hsiung-nu continued to tyrannize the entire border region, the Chinese, in turn, perpetuated the violence by repopulating any region that the Hsiung-nu had decimated, using people as an almost inexhaustible natural resource.

Eventually, when the casualties inflicted by the nomad raiders had become too staggering, the Chinese rulers decided that they had no alternative but to deal with the Hsiung-nu directly at a government level. The Chinese had to buy peace from the horsemen in hard money, and finally they had to allocate as much as 7 per cent of their annual revenue to keep the marauders from raiding their land. As a proportion of the nation's wealth the cash value of each year's payment is estimated to have been the equivalent of $40 million in modern money—paid to the Hsiung-nu chieftains in pure gold. And even at this staggering cost, tranquillity was not assured.

For centuries to come, other horsemen of the no-

madization would continue to be cast from much the same mold as the Scythians, Sarmatians, Yueh-Chi and Hsiung-nu. To look upon the Hun, who in the Fifth Century A.D. thrust westward out of the steppes to contribute to the fall of Rome, or the Mongol cavalrymen of Genghis Khan and Tamerlane, who terrorized China, India, the Near East and eastern Europe in the 13th and 14th centuries, is to rediscover in many ways the essential Scythian described by Herodotus centuries before.

Equally enduring were the forces that triggered the eruptions of mounted hordes from within the steppes into the settled world outside. These invasions grew ever more spectacular as time went on. Even in the early years, the recurring push-and-shove of tribes competing for choice pasture land had an effect resembling that of a combination billiard shot. For instance, after the Hsiung-nu drove the Yueh-Chi westward from the Gobi region in the Second Century B.C., the Yueh-Chi were attacked by a horde called the Wu-Sun and forced southwest into Bactria, a Greek kingdom centered in what today is northern Afghanistan. There the Yueh-Chi displaced other nomadic tribesmen known as the Sakas, who, as a result, entered a part of eastern Persia then called Parthia and mixed with its inhabitants, spawning a people who later subdued part of western India.

Most likely it was a similar situation that originally dislodged the Scythians from their pasturage in an obscure homeland and ultimately thrust them into south Russia and so into the awareness of the world. And it was precisely the same sort of phenomenon that signaled the beginning of the end of the once-powerful Scythians.

Their days were already numbered when bands of

The Great Wall, built by the Chinese to protect their northern frontier from plundering Hsiung-nu horsemen, snakes for more than 2,000 miles across China. In places the wall rises to 30 feet and spreads 25 feet at the base. Built in sections, the massive brick-and-stone-faced bulwark was begun in the Fourth Century B.C. and was linked together in 214 B.C.; repairs and additions continued for several hundred years.

neighboring Sarmatians began crossing over the Don into south Russia in the Fourth Century B.C. The strife that ensued forced some Scythians to move west into what is today Rumania, where they formed a short-lived kingdom known to classical writers as Little Scythia. Meantime, Scythians who remained north of the Black Sea mingled with the invaders, and in time both groups joined forces to ward off their enemies, including later waves of Sarmatians.

As the Sarmatians began encroaching more and more on the south Russian steppe, the Scythians, who had once humiliated Darius and his army of 700,000 men, yielded. They were not the same forceful people they had been at their height of power in the Fifth Century B.C. Through the years they had succumbed increasingly to opulence, and during the process had lost the vigor that once characterized them. Indeed, most of them had abandoned the nomadic way of life and settled down in cities.

By the Second Century B.C. invading Sarmatians had forced the once-mighty masters of the steppe into the Crimea. There the surviving Scythians managed to establish another kingdom, the ruins of whose capital, Neapolis, cover some 40 acres near the present-day city of Simferopol. Enclosed by a massive stone wall, the city contained impressive public buildings, with Greek-style columns and marble statuary, and private houses with mural-covered walls.

This new Crimean kingdom, ruled by urbanized horsemen, was powerful enough to pose a serious threat to Mithradates the Great, King of Pontus in Asia Minor. Alarmed, Mithradates sent an expedition against them and vanquished them in 106 B.C. Soon after their final defeat the Scythians vanished entirely as a distinct people. They would be virtually forgotten for many centuries to come, overshadowed by other hordes of the enduring, ever-fermenting people of the nomadization who rode out to command the attention and to affect the destinies of waxing and waning civilizations all around the steppes.

An Artistic Zoo—
the Menagerie
of the Horsemen

On a half-inch-high plaque, a panther attacks an animal that is part horse, part eagle, part lion; its antlers and tail form birds' heads.

History is indebted to Greek metalsmiths for the only visual record of the life style and appearance of the first horsemen. But much of what survives of the ancient nomads' own creative handiwork consists of tiny sculptures of animals fashioned in bronze and in gold. Although thousands of such ornaments have been found as far apart as China and Germany, they are so similar in mood and execution that scholars call them by one name: the Animal Style.

The commonest subjects are felines and birds of prey—often combined into griffins—stags, horses, ibexes and occasionally fish. Sometimes the animals are presented singly; sometimes two are shown locked in combat. Often one creature grows, as if by magic, out of the body of another. And all exude such an aura of muscular tension and sensory alertness that they seem about to spring into action.

Obviously these objects had a deep significance for their owners, though scholars can only conjecture about that meaning, drawing on their knowledge of modern Eurasian tribes, who have hardly changed in over 2,000 years. For these people, like the first horsemen, nature's forces are inextricably tied to the animals of the wild.

Again and Again, the Stag

The stag is a common theme in the art of the steppe riders, but it turns up most frequently in the work of the Scythians. Whether an elk, red deer or reindeer, the stag is nearly always portrayed with a lordly display of antlers—their tines often forming the heads of other creatures—flowing down from the animal's outstretched head and over its back. Besides the Scythians, other nomads seem to have felt a special affinity with the stag; the Sakas of Central Asia, some scholars believe, adopted it as their tribal emblem.

Once part of a ceremonial pole, this five-inch bronze elk from Mongolia conveys the majesty the horsemen so admired in the animal.

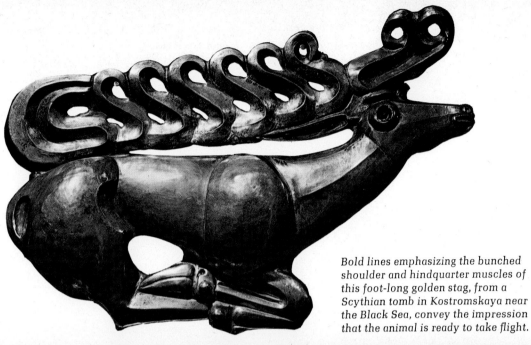

Bold lines emphasizing the bunched
shoulder and hindquarter muscles of
this foot-long golden stag, from a
Scythian tomb in Kostromskaya near
the Black Sea, convey the impression
that the animal is ready to take flight.

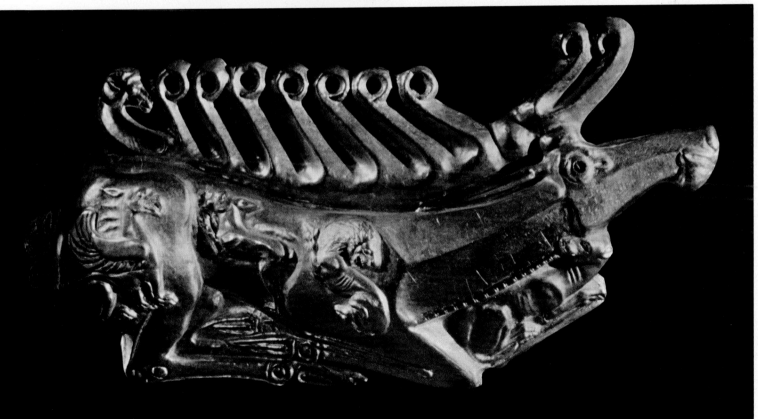

From the Scythian tomb at Kul Oba, a 12-inch stag,
embellished with other animals, was made
by a Greek craftsman to Scythian specifications.
Although the goldsmith followed his instructions, he
failed to capture the vitality of the find pictured
above. Both stags were used as shield ornaments.

In Admiration of Cats

Swift, lithe and powerful, the big cats of the open steppes were an ever-present danger to the nomads and their flocks. Lions, tigers, leopards and panthers all roamed the grasslands of Eurasia. In their art, the nomads portrayed felines with their teeth and powerful muscles almost always exaggerated, and their bodies often contorted in tense positions to emphasize the beasts' ferocity. Scholars generally agree that when a horseman wore a plaque bearing images of such fearsome beasts, he himself hoped to acquire the creatures' admired attributes.

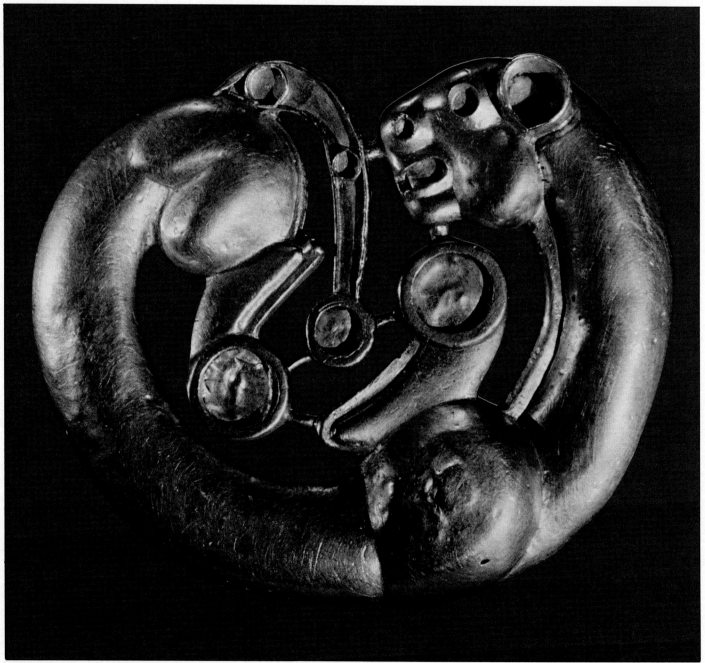

A gold lioness four inches across, from the Altai Mountains, curls nose-to-tail in a full circle. The round holes once held colored inlays.

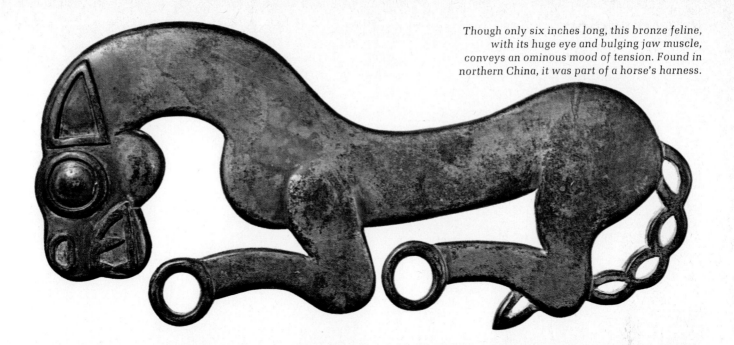

Though only six inches long, this bronze feline, with its huge eye and bulging jaw muscle, conveys an ominous mood of tension. Found in northern China, it was part of a horse's harness.

The paws and tail of this 15-inch-long panther evolve into 10 tiny felines. Although the plaque, which once adorned a warrior's armor, comes from Kelermes, east of the Crimea, the flexed posture echoes that of the example at left from Pazyryk, more than 2,000 miles away.

An ibex cowers beneath sweeping curves that suggest a looming bird on this ceremonial pole top found at Ulski, near the Black Sea.

Homage to Birds of Prey

In Animal Style art some birds of prey are highly realistic, down to the feather details, but other designs incorporate abstract swirls or curving lines, so that just a beak and an eye may symbolize the whole. Most frequently the birds figure in impossible situations like the one below, in which an eagle assaults a full-grown and virtually invulnerable yak. To experts, such fanciful vignettes confirm that birds of prey, whose soaring silhouettes were a common sight on the steppes, held a spiritual significance for the horsemen that was larger than real life.

On a six-inch-long gold buckle inlaid with turquoise, one of a pair found in Siberia, a monstrous eagle grasps in its beak a weakened yak. Underneath the eagle, a snarling lion (at far right) seems to be participating in the fray. And at the lion's throat the clutching fingers of a man's hand are visible.

A Taste for Bloody Combat

Combat between the natural enemies of the steppes is a theme repeated again and again in the nomads' art. The fight may be between two equally matched animals, but more often the scene involves a predator —sometimes an imaginary composite of bird and beast of prey— swooping down mercilessly upon a defenseless victim to kill and devour. The savage scenes vividly reflect one of the harshest continuing realities of steppe life: weaker animals, both the tamed and the untamed, made easy prey for the great beasts of the wild.

On a five-inch-long piece from Siberia, a catlike beast with stylized wings sinks its fangs into a horselike creature. The configurations of Animal Style art—rounded shapes, interlocked bodies —derive partly from the need to compress large subjects onto small items worn as ornaments.

A giant snake is coiled in deadly battle with a wolf in this six-inch-long Siberian plaque. The ornament was once inlaid with colorful stones or enamel; the holes along its edges indicate that it was once stitched to a horseman's apparel.

A striped tiger, whose long tail has broken off, stretches wide its powerful jaws to engulf a newborn calf. The three-inch-long bronze plaque was found in Mongolia.

A Life-giving Golden Guardian

Though the fish is a rare subject in Animal Style art, examples have been discovered in sites as widely separated as Siberia and Germany. The spectacular example below was turned up in Vettersfelde, near Brandenburg, in 1882, along with the complete battle gear of a Scythian chief. How the equipment got there can only be conjectured: it may have been a gift; it may have been traded, or stolen by grave robbers. Some experts believe the Scythians associated fish with a deity who was the guardian spirit of their most prized possessions—their horses.

Fashioned in gold by a Greek craftsman who was far more
at home with the Animal Style than the Greek creator
of the stag on page 89, this 16-inch-long fish represents the
epitome of nomad art. A teeming world of other beasts
—felines in combat with a boar, a deer, a spread-winged eagle
and a school of fish following a man-headed leader, who
looks like a Scythian—fills the great fish's body. Even its tail
has been transformed into two magisterial rams' heads.

Chapter Four: Treasures and Thieves

How could a people as dynamic as the Scythians become almost completely forgotten? They left no written records to save them from oblivion. Except for Herodotus' account and a few references to them by other writers, their existence might never have been known at all. And even Herodotus was doubted. A century or so after his death, he was derided by no less a detractor than Aristotle as a "legend-monger." As a result, Herodotus' tales about the wealth and violence, the exuberance and power of the Scythians seemed substantiating evidence of his weakness for fables. Never mind that the man who had been called by Cicero the Father of History knew the Scythians firsthand. Who, after all, could believe that these hard-drinking, rough-and-tumble tribesmen of the steppes had the grace and sophistication to bury their dead chieftains in such prodigal style?

As things turned out, however, it was precisely through their spectacular burials that the Scythians and similar nonliterate horsemen would speak convincingly to posterity. They and their brethren left behind thousands of large and small mounds to mark the graves of honored dead—all the way from the Ukraine to the Altai Mountains of Siberia and beyond. Moreover, their tombs have revealed a side of them that Herodotus and other ancient commentators failed to report: these devastating warriors on horseback also produced art of stunning force and vitality.

The indigenous art of the Scythians, along with that of other steppe nomads, is labeled the Animal Style, underscoring the artists' preoccupation with beasts, mostly wild or fantastic. Stags, leopards, eagles and various creatures, some engaged in mortal combat, appear on finely made gold plaques that the horsemen attached to their clothing, belt plates, bridles and other accouterments.

The Scythians also had a well-developed taste for Greek art. Some of the most lavishly ornamented gold and silver bowls, sword hilts and scabbards, bracelets and diadems found in their tombs appear to have been the work of craftsmen living in the Greek trading colonies along the shores of the Black Sea. The best of these pieces may well have been imports from the Greek homeland itself.

The rediscovery of the Scythians began more than 200 years ago with rich finds such as these, but not until the 20th Century did a picture of their rise to supremacy and their place in the whole nomadic society of the steppes of eastern Europe and Asia come into sharp focus. In fact, as recently as the 1960s and 1970s, some indispensable pieces of the Scythian puzzle were recovered. At the same time, knowledge of the other horsemen of the steppes—who, as archeology has demonstrated, were similar to Scythians in many respects—has also been widely expanded. In the case of the mounted Altai tribesmen and their frozen tombs, it may even be more complete.

The most recent—and one of the richest—of Scythian finds was made during the summer of 1971 by a team of Soviet archeologists in the southern Ukraine. The site, a burial mound that reached 35 feet into the sky from a flat landscape of wheat fields, lay in an area where a great deal of construction was about to begin. Aided by funds from the Soviet government

Nose-to-nose over a horn-shaped vessel, two Scythians pledge everlasting brotherhood by drinking drops of blood mixed with wine. This Fourth Century B.C. gold plaque, discovered in a burial mound at Kul Olba in the Crimea, exemplifies the tomb treasures that not only confirm the wealth of these horsemen, but also shed light on their dress and customs.

and modern equipment, the archeologists managed to complete their excavations in a record six months. They used bulldozers to clear away the mound itself and expose whatever lay underneath. While the bulldozers roared back and forth, the archeologists kept a sharp eye out to be certain that the machines did not sweep away any valuable relics.

Once the 2,400-year-old mound had been leveled, the archeologists set about removing the dirt that had filled a shaft leading to a tomb. When finally they reached the bottom, some 20 feet below ground level, they faced the jumbled ruins of a wooden funeral carriage, and behind a spoked wheel, the first of several skeletons—apparently that of the driver.

The excavators knew at once that they were onto something unusual: an unplundered tomb. (The last unplundered Scythian tomb to have been explored had been found in 1912, almost half a century before.) And indeed, the site lived up to the archeologists' wildest expectations. The scientists made one dazzling discovery after another, including the skeleton of a woman described as a princess, who was surrounded and covered by a golden treasure (page 23). She had been sealed away in the tomb's cool darkness wearing a gold headpiece, earrings, a necklace, 11 rings, three armbands—and a gown stitched with gold plaques.

Alongside the princess, in an alabaster sarcophagus lined with wood, lay the bones of a one-and-a-half-year-old girl, doubtless her daughter, who had been laid to rest wearing much the same jewelry as her mother—only in miniature. The child's sarcophagus had been brought into the tomb through a separate entrance, leading the archeologists to surmise that the girl had been buried some time after

An insatiable collector, Czar Peter the Great designed and built an imperial museum, which included a Cabinet of Curiosities. There he exhibited not only malformed human bodies and a personal collection of arms and art but also, fortunately for history, much of the gold treasure taken in the early 18th Century from prehistoric Siberian graves.

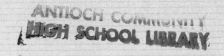

her mother, who perhaps had died giving birth to her.

Close by the bones of the princess and child were the remains of a powerfully built young man, about 18 years old, with quiver and bow at hand. He may well have been an arms bearer, dispatched to defend the princess in the life after death. That he was sacrificed, perhaps by strangulation, was a fact gruesomely evident to the archeologists: his fingers had clawed into the earth in his final agony. Also sacrificed for the princess' benefit was a young woman, possibly a cook; in a niche next to her skeleton lay bronze cooking vessels and the remains of food. The archeologists came upon yet another pathetic victim in a side corridor: an eight-year-old girl, who may have served as a messenger.

As exciting as these discoveries were, still greater ones were in the offing. In a separate grave, beneath the base of the mound that had once covered the princess' tomb, excavators came upon the scattered bones of a man of about 50, presumably her husband. The way in which the bones had been tossed about clearly indicated to the archeologists that robbers, perhaps only a short time after the man had been placed there, had tunneled into the tomb, ransacked it and carried off its treasure. But patient digging soon revealed that the plunderers had left behind three priceless pieces: a gold-wrapped whip, a sword with its gold-plated hilt protruding from a gold scabbard and—most spectacular of all—a golden pectoral, or breastplate, weighing two and a half pounds *(page 33)*. How had these treasures escaped the robbers' notice? Part of the tomb may have caved in before the thieves actually entered it, and the resulting earth slide may have buried the pieces.

The pectoral, the most exciting Scythian find in years, was the work of a Greek master goldsmith who composed it of three curving friezelike bands, one above the other. On the uppermost band four Scythians, surrounded by their cattle, sheep and horses, go about such peaceful tasks as milking a ewe and working on what appears to be a woolly shirt. Their animals graze contentedly, nurse their young or idly lift a hind foot to scratch a flank. Every detail of the men's costumes, every lock of their hair, every streak in the animals' fur is rendered with exquisite, lifelike precision. Below the middle band, which has a curling floral pattern, the mood changes abruptly. The third band boils with the combative animal action that is so characteristically Scythian. Griffins, horses, a lion, a leopard and other creatures furiously attack one another. All of these figures—the four men and 44 animals—were first cast in gold and then welded to the pectoral's framework.

Because of the interest aroused by the pectoral and other finds, the site is being converted into a sort of open-air museum. The earth mound, leveled by the bulldozers, is to be rebuilt to its original 35-foot height, and an opening left in it in order to allow visitors to descend into the graves through concrete-reinforced shafts.

Such vital elements in re-creating the horsemen's story, long buried in the darkness of the earth, might have been wholly destroyed or at least irreparably damaged had it not been for a fiat by Peter the Great, Czar of all the Russias, early in the 18th Century.

The mounted nomads had made no attempt to hide their burials. Rather, trusting each other not to disturb the resting places of their dead, they made them as conspicuous as possible by heaping up mounds of

Elaborate Burials for Men and Horses

Beneath large earthen mounds—some, like the one at right, with a circumference of more than a thousand feet—the Scythians of the Black Sea region buried their chieftains along with hoards of gold and richly caparisoned riding horses. Rising in plain view above the steppe, such mounds were, over the centuries, irresistible magnets for grave robbers, and nearly all the tombs excavated had been seriously damaged by plunderers in search of treasure. In a few cases, however, shown by the pair of graves diagramed at far right, the tombs had never before been entered, or else were sufficiently intact to give the excavators an idea of the plans, and of the original positions of their human and animal occupants.

At Alexandropol in the Ukraine a burial mound, some 60 feet high, dwarfs the hay wagon in this 19th Century etching. When excavated, the mound revealed a man's grave, which had been looted, and a passage holding the bones of 14 horses, some of which still wore harnesses rich with gold and silver.

dirt or stones, or both, over the graves. Called *kurgans* in Russian, they exist in clusters all across the steppes. There are some 100,000 barrows in the Ukraine alone. In the Minusinsk area of Siberia, as far as the eye can see the terrain is one gigantic graveyard. From the vantage point of a mountaintop, Austrian historian Gero von Merhart contemplated the scene during World War I:

"Here, at our feet, we can see the first cemetery in a lonely dip high on the mountainside we have climbed: mound after mound, in an irregular mass, each encompassed by weathered stones, with slabs—thin, but broad and tall, often of grotesque shape, depending upon the way they chanced to break; some have fallen to the ground, others are cracked and crumbling, but most of them still stand boldly, massed together in this valley of death like a petrified herd of mysterious dark red animals. We seek to bring some order into this confusion, and to count them: there are more than 100 mounds in a single narrow space, none of them less than ten square meters [33 square feet] in extent, and many several times as big. And down there, at the foot of the mountain, we glimpse another, and a second, and yet a third field of barrows . . . and then more *kurgans*, scattered far and wide across the plain."

Throughout the centuries such barrows were a source of almost everything but enlightenment. By Czar Peter the Great's time, fable, legend and superstition had grown up around them, but to the fearless and irreverent, the hulking mounds loomed as standing invitations to steal.

It was, in fact, the large-scale plundering of the graves deep inside the mounds that eventually brought these monuments of the horsemen's past to Peter's attention and set the stage for the rediscov-

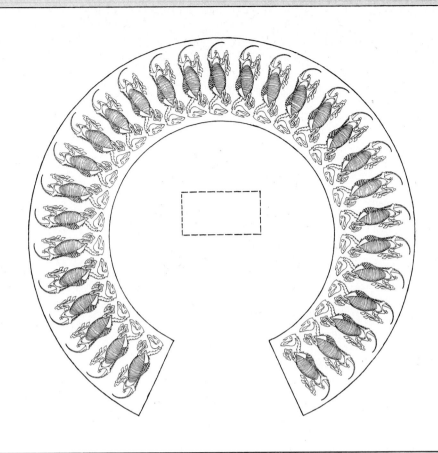

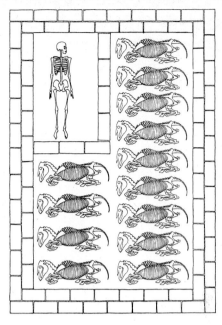

In a mound in the Caucasus, skeletons
of 29 horses were found arranged in
a circular trench (left) surrounding the
ransacked grave of their master.
Another tomb (above) in the same area
was almost entirely filled with
the neatly aligned bodies of 13 horses.

ery of the Scythians and other mounted nomadic peoples. In 1715 Peter and Czarina Catherine received an amazing collection of ancient golden plaques, medallions, buckles and coins as a gift commemorating the birth of their first son. The treasure, stripped from burial mounds somewhere in Siberia, had been assembled by the donor, Nikita Demidov, a man who had started life as a blacksmith and wound up as one of the richest mineowners in the Urals, as well as a companion of Peter's in some of the Czar's notorious drinking bouts. Demidov's gift, appraised for its gold weight alone, came to some 100,000 rubles, a substantial sum of money even for a man as rich as the Czar.

What intrigued Peter and his court, however, was not so much the extravagance of Demidov's gesture, as the masterful, dynamic rendering of the animals on the various pieces. Many seethed with fury: a wolf struggling in the coils of a serpent; a horse and a feline, their bodies twisting in a life-death struggle; a falcon-like bird grasping a swan in its cruel talons.

The Czar was dismayed when he learned that similarly beautiful pieces were being regularly taken from Siberian graves and melted down. He promptly issued orders to put an end to this destruction and demanded that thenceforth such relics be turned over to the crown. In response, the governor of Siberia amassed and dispatched to Peter 90 gold objects weighing almost 60 pounds. This collection, together with Demidov's earlier lavish present, became the nucleus of the "Siberian Gold Treasure of Peter the Great," today one of the glittering showpieces of Leningrad's Hermitage Museum. By the time of Peter's death in 1725, the treasure included an immense diversity of plaques—some as big as a man's hand —buckles, collars and plates, almost all stamped

Secrets of the Frozen Tombs

When the archeologist Sergei Rudenko opened the tombs in the Pazyryk Valley of Siberia's Altai Mountains, he found that they, too, had been robbed. But unlike the barrows erected by the Black Sea Scythians, the Siberian tombs—by the very fact that they had been looted—yielded a treasure that was priceless because of the light it shed on the ways of the steppe nomads. The temperature inside the rock-covered log tombs had dropped below freezing, and moisture, entering through the shafts dug by the grave robbers, had turned to ice. Thus the tombs became frozen storehouses, in which the bodies of tribal chieftains, their women, horses and possessions of perishable fur, fabric, leather and wood were preserved for all time.

Rudenko's workers remove the logs covering a tomb during a 1949 excavation. In the partially ice-filled chamber beneath, the bodies of a man and a woman lay in a long coffin, and scattered about were items as diverse as a pigtail and cheese.

with the increasingly familiar Animal Style motifs.

Though more and more of these priceless curiosities came to light as the 18th Century progressed, no one could say with any certainty who had made them. And now they were beginning to turn up not only in Siberia but in south Russia as well. In 1763, General Alexis Melgunov, on military duty in the Ukraine, decided to investigate some of the huge mounds that broke the monotony of the otherwise flat landscape between the Bug and Dnieper rivers. He set about excavating one of them. Although his methods and record keeping were to cause subsequent archeologists to gnash their teeth, he unearthed a breathtakingly magnificent golden hoard. In addition to objects embellished with animals, it included several pieces of excellent Greek workmanship.

The hoard was sent to Catherine the Great, who now sat on the throne. It caused a stir in court, and since Catherine maintained extensive diplomatic relations with the nations of western Europe, word spread to French and German scholars, setting off a spate of digging in south Russia. A link was established between the finds and the riders described by Herodotus. Had not the historian indicated that the Scythians maintained close contact with the Greek cities on the shores of the Black Sea? And here in the graves of these long-forgotten people were pieces of Greek craftsmanship and origin.

Excavations carried out in south Russia during the first half of the 19th Century were more often than not unscientific. Only after 1859, when the Imperial Russian Archeological Commission was founded, did the study of the tombs proceed in methodical fashion. By then it had long been accepted that the south Russian tombs belonged to the Scythians, and as more and more evidence of the grandiose manner in

How nature and grave looters inadvertently worked together to safeguard the perishable contents of the Altai burial sites is explained in this cross section of one of the tombs. The tomb chamber itself, walled and roofed with logs, lay at the bottom of a pit 15 feet deep. Earth from the pit was spread at ground level to form a low mound, which was then topped by piles of boulders. Cold winter air, settling in the spaces between the stones, stayed frigid during the brief mountain summers, so that a section of earth around the burial chamber (gray) became perpetually frozen. To reach the tomb, the grave robbers removed some of the boulders, dug down to the tomb's roof and hacked their way through it. As water seeped through the opening, it covered the grave's contents and congealed into ice. In time dirt and stones plugged the hole.

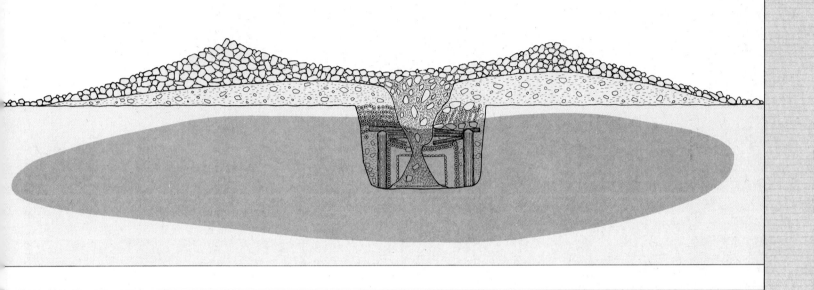

which they buried their leaders accumulated, scholars realized that Herodotus had indeed been telling the truth. At the same time, the lavishness of the grave goods established beyond doubt that the Scythians had been men of power who must have had control of the extremely profitable trade that passed through their domain.

As they waxed rich, the Scythians indulged a passion not just for golden objects but also for Greek works that portrayed them in various familiar activities. They could not have anticipated the excitement such pieces would produce centuries later. For here in gold and silver on the sides of vases and bowls are their physical features, their clothing, their equipment, their animals—a visual record almost as precise and as lively as a photograph.

Some of the individual Greek works have achieved special celebrity among students of art and archeology; a quick-label reference to them without description in scholarly texts is sufficient to conjure up a vivid and detailed image in the minds of the experts. For example, a gold comb taken from a barrow at Solokha on the lower Dnieper in 1912 is customarily referred to simply as the Solokha comb. To the layman the name may be meaningless; yet when one sees the comb (page 38) and remembers its origin, one cannot help but be staggered by the beauty of its execution. Adorning the top are two Scythian warriors on foot, fighting a mounted warrior wearing Grecian armor —a scene executed in such startling detail that even the blood flowing from the neck wound of a fallen horse is visible.

Other Greek-made pieces are as graphic—and as beautiful. A silver and gilt amphora (page 30) discovered in 1862 in a grave at a site called Chertomlyk, also on the Dnieper, bears in relief on its gleaming

Six wooden poles from a grave site at Pazyryk provided the frame for a Fifth Century B.C. felt-covered tent into which Altai horsemen went to inhale the intoxicating vapors of hemp.

To produce the narcotic fumes inside the tent, stones were heated in a fire and placed in vessels such as those above; hemp seeds were then liberally scattered over the stones. These bronze pots, also found at Pazyryk, contained stones and charred hemp seeds.

surface a group of Scythians who could be American wranglers: one is roping a shaggy-maned steed, another is removing hobbles from a saddled horse. Around the lustrous surface of an electrum vase (page 34) excavated in a *kurgan* at Kul Oba in the Crimea in 1875, two Scythians converse, a third adjusts a bow string and a fourth, with reaching fingers and an intent look, explores the ailing tooth, or perhaps the mouth wound, of a companion.

Similar pieces of Greek origin have continued to ·turn up in Scythian graves; the spectacular golden pectoral found in the Ukraine in 1971 is only one of them. In 1969 a young Soviet archeologist, Vasili Bidzilya, was given the routine assignment of exploring some burial mounds on the lower Dnieper that were threatened by a new irrigation project. In one of the mounds he uncovered a gold and silver loving cup (page 29), bearing figures that Soviet historian Alexander Kirpichnikov calls "probably the finest portraits of Scythians in existence."

On one side of the cup sit two long-haired, bearded men. Clutching whips, both are wearing full-length tunics, or caftans, of patterned fabric, and tight leather boots secured at the ankles with thongs. Around the waist of one man is a sword belt; the other man holds a quiver of arrows, and a bow case and bow rest beside him. On the opposite side of the cup, unfortunately damaged, is a group of men, among them two seated and beardless figures, each with an arm outstretched toward the other; a goblet rests on the knee of one. To their left can be discerned a figure drinking from a wineskin. The hands and faces of all the figures are in silver and their garments in gold, providing a luminous, lifelike effect.

This gold and silver cup, however, was only one of the magnificent treasures that Bidzilya recovered from the Dnieper graves and delivered to Dr. Boris Piotrovsky, Director of the Hermitage Museum. As reported by the historian Kirpichnikov, the director's "eyes widened as, one after another, gold-rimmed vases, a gold-and-silver bowl, two drinking horns embellished with gold and silver, three silver vessels and a bundle containing hundreds of small gold discs were placed on his desk."

Such finds paint a picture of the Scythians' immense wealth. But the mounds alone would be enough to suggest the horsemen's power. The *kurgan* at Chertomlyk is one of the most impressive. The Scythians built it 60 feet high (the height of a six-story building), with a base 1,100 feet around, and encircled it with stones. The mound was approached by a kind of alley made with more stones.

When archeologists excavated the Chertomlyk site in 1862, they disclosed a subterranean tomb complex that could only have been dug with as much toil as had gone into the construction of the towering mound itself. The Scythians had first cut a large vertical shaft that measured 15 by 7 feet at the top and that gradually expanded like a long, narrow cone as it descended to a depth of about 36 feet. The broad bottom of the shaft formed the main burial chamber, and here lay the fragments of a chieftain's empty coffin. Four other chambers opened off it, and a passageway through one led through to yet another and larger chamber whose purpose is still unknown.

Three chambers contained the skeletons of four minions of the chief's personal household, while the fourth housed those of the chieftain's concubine and her armed attendant. The concubine had been placed on a couch whose traces still bore signs of green, yellow and blue paint. On her forehead rested a band of gold plates wrought in the shape of flowers. Earrings with gold pendants rested at each side of her skull. Her neck was still encircled by a solid gold torque with lion finials. Gold-ribbed bracelets circled each arm, and on every finger was a gold ring—one of them adorned with a duck in flight. The outline of her form was evoked by 57 square gold plaques that had once glittered on a purple dress, or shroud, of which only shreds survived.

The jewelry worn by the woman was overshadowed by the other finds. The famous silver and gilt amphora with its frieze of Scythian horse wranglers was the most stunning piece of a vast and dazzling treasure. From the various chambers came masses of gold ornaments—plaques, buttons, bands, cylinders, pendants, bracelets, torques. Some 2,500 pieces were taken from one chamber alone. From another came a golden plate from a bow case depicting scenes from Greek mythology, a sword with its hilt plated with

A Gift from the Past in Perishable Wood

Exposed to the elements, wood disintegrates quickly—and so, ancient wooden artifacts rarely turn up whole in archeological digs. But in Siberia, in the frozen tombs of the Altai horsemen, a variety of carved figures survived more than two millennia to delight the 20th Century eye. Recovered still clinging to crumbling leather horse gear, the pieces display not only a high degree of skill, but the woodcarvers' ability to capture unerringly, though often with a whimsical eye, their subjects' essence.

With curving leather horns and a body overlaid with gold foil, a wide-eyed ram from a Fourth Century B.C. bridle measures less than three inches long.

Sprouting a horn from its beak, the so-called fantastic bird may well have been a crest for a horse's mask. Only fragments remain of the gold foil that once covered the eight-inch head.

A grinning three-toed cat, three and a half inches long, is one of eight similar reclining felines with short round ears that decorated a leather bridle.

The curling horn of a three-inch-long profile of a mountain sheep was fashioned from a piece of thick leather.

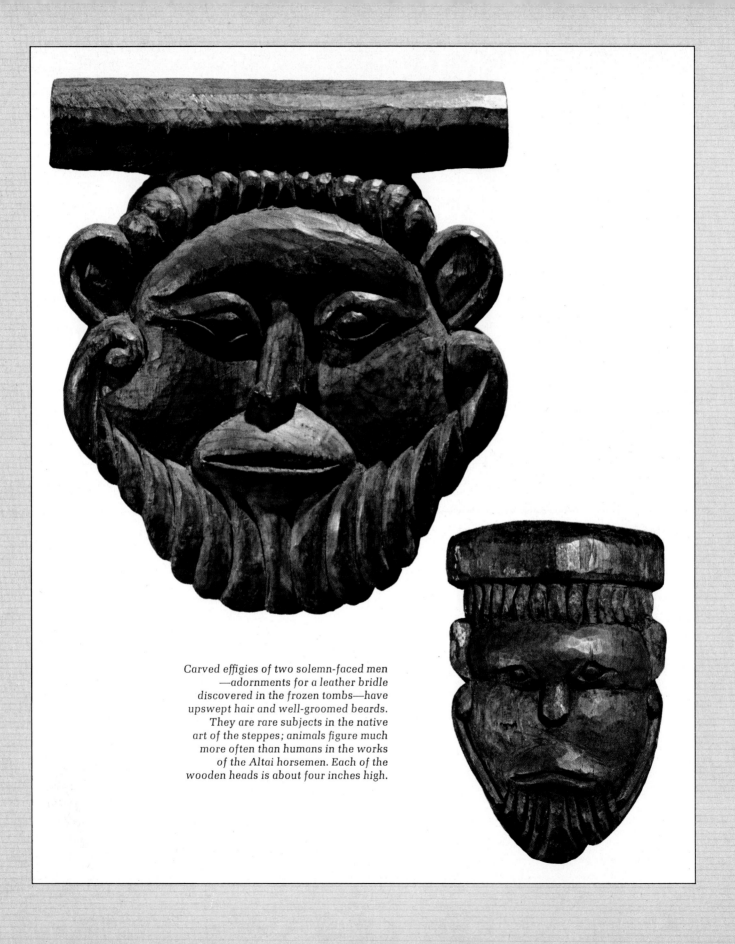

Carved effigies of two solemn-faced men —adornments for a leather bridle discovered in the frozen tombs—have upswept hair and well-groomed beards. They are rare subjects in the native art of the steppes; animals figure much more often than humans in the works of the Altai horsemen. Each of the wooden heads is about four inches high.

gold, and 700 gold plaques. Numerous amphorae and cooking cauldrons made of bronze were also recovered, as well as whetstones and whip handles—these, too, embellished with gold. The archeologists gathered up bronze arrowheads by the hundreds, along with spearheads, swords and standards decorated with animal shapes—and mixed in with these assorted bronze objects were iron knife blades. And in three pits, each about nine feet square, the excavators uncovered the remains of 11 horses with gold and silver bridle ornaments; nearby were buried two grooms, each with a quiver full of arrows.

But treasure was only part of the archeologists' find. The tomb had been entered in ancient times by robbers who, with beeline accuracy, had tunneled into the mound—right into the largest chamber—and there, after rifling the chieftain's coffin at the bottom of the central shaft and scattering his bones about, had assembled some of the valuables for removal. But their looting was cut short by a cave-in that buried one of the robbers along with his six-wick oil lamp and doubtless sent his confederates scrambling on their hands and knees to safety. Had the plundering not been so drastically terminated, the entire contents of the mound would have been lost—and the modern world's knowledge of the Scythians would have been incomparably poorer.

Grave robbing was a venerable profession, one that began in ancient times and continued right up to the 20th Century. Evidently the technique of grave robbing developed right along with the technique of constructing ever more elaborate tombs. Many sites were deftly entered soon after the burials took place. The Chertomlyk barrow seems to have been one of those that were quickly despoiled. The looters may even have been among the workmen who helped dig the tomb and pile up the barrow or among those set to guard the tomb.

By Peter the Great's time, grave robbing had reached an astonishing level of professionalism, and *kurgans* were being ruthlessly pillaged. In the part of Siberia where the Austrian scholar Von Merhart had seen fields of barrows "scattered far and wide across the plain," a class of grave robbers known as the *bugrovshchiki* (mound diggers) came close to being organized as an industry.

"The *bugrovshchiki* . . . handed down from father to son their skill in a craft that they regarded as wholly respectable," says the German scholar Karl Jettmar in his book, *Art of the Steppes*. They could determine from the sizes of the mounds which of them were the ones likely to contain treasure, and from their knowledge of how such barrows were constructed, "they calculated exactly in which direction the shaft had to be dug in order to strike the treasure. No wonder that at that time there was a regular market price for plundered Siberian gold."

Though the chances today of finding intact the grave of a wealthy steppe horseman are almost nil, even the tombs that long ago were ripped open can offer astounding finds—as the frozen tombs of Siberia have excitingly demonstrated. The most renowned lie in the Pazyryk Valley in the Altai Mountains, just north of Siberia's border with Mongolia. According to Sergei Ivanovich Rudenko, the Soviet archeologist who excavated the Pazyryk tombs first in 1929 and again after the war, from 1947 to 1949, they form the Fourth Century B.C. cemetery of a community of horsemen who closely resembled the Black Sea Scythians in their "way of life, occupation, dress, weapons and other aspects of material culture."

The preservation of the tombs came about as the result of a happy combination of factors: the way in which the graves were constructed, the climate of the area and the zeal of the robbers in entering the burial chambers. Although the tombs lie well south of the Siberian tundra, where the subsoil is permanently frozen, the boulders that were heaped on top of them by the horsemen prevented the spring sun from thawing the frost-bound earth underneath. At the same time the frigid air of the severe Altai winter settled through the interstices of the boulders and turned the chambers below—walled and roofed with notched and fitted logs—into natural refrigerators. The freezing within the tombs set in gradually—not fast enough to prevent the decay of food buried with the dead, but quickly enough to preserve the skin and hair of some of the corpses in an astonishingly lifelike state. Later, after the entry of the robbers, rain and moisture condensed from the air trickled down through the openings left by the intruders and into these subterranean log cabins, and then froze around bodies, garments, horse gear and other items. Thus these mementos of the horsemen came to be locked away in the glassy ice, as though in a time capsule, waiting to be examined 2,400 years later.

Not all the Pazyryk bodies were well preserved, but those that were provided information that otherwise would never have been obtained concerning the mounted nomads. If Rudenko had found only skeletons, he would have known that the chieftains were exceptionally tall and strong and that racially the Altai tribesmen were predominantly of European type, with a few of Mongoloid stock mixed in. But bones alone could not have told Rudenko such personal details as the length of a nose or hair color. At least one man had black wavy hair and one woman a luxuriant soft pile of dark chestnut tresses.

Among the frozen dead was the body of a sturdily built chieftain, a man in his sixties who, perhaps to emphasize his rank, had had himself covered with tattoos—a veritable gallery of animal art at its strangest, with real and imaginary beasts stalking, pouncing, crouching, fleeing (page 113). The chieftain's left breast bore the head of a griffin, whose body twined under his left arm and up over his shoulder, its long, raised, twisting tail ending in the head of a bird, or perhaps a snake. On his right arm was a fantastic processional consisting of an onager, a winged monster, a horned ram, a deer with an eagle's beak and long antlers that turn into bird heads, and a looming, fanged carnivore. On the man's left arm were two deer and a mountain goat. A fish spanned the length of his shin from knee to ankle, and below it, wrapped around his foot, curled a fanged, horned monster with a feline tail and three birds on its neck.

The chieftain, like the other Altai dead, had been carefully embalmed. The process involved removing brains and viscera, as well as sections of muscle; Rudenko theorized that the muscle tissue may have been consumed in cannibalistic rites; he based this possibility on Herodotus' account of the Issedonians, one of the Scythians' neighboring tribes who ritualistically ate the flesh of their dead. After the bodies had been properly prepared, they were stuffed with grass, moss and herbs and the incisions closed with stitches of hair or tendon. The heads were partially or completely shaved, as were the faces of the men. Shaving the heads apparently made it easier to ex-

Frozen solid for more than 2,000 years, the body of a 60-year-old chieftain, recovered in 1947 from a burial mound high in the Altai Mountains of south-central Siberia, bore elaborate tattoos (right, top and bottom). The designs—created by pricking the skin and rubbing soot into the perforations—formed a menagerie of real and imaginary beasts that curled round the arms, across the chest and the back, and up one leg. Dots tattooed along the spine (right, bottom) may have been placed there to ease back pain. The photograph below is a slightly enlarged detail from the chieftain's right arm, and shows a prancing deer with long antlers and an eagle's beak.

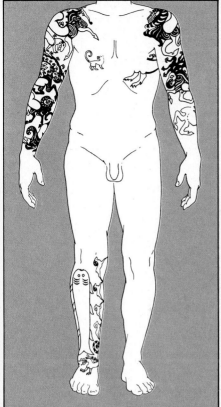

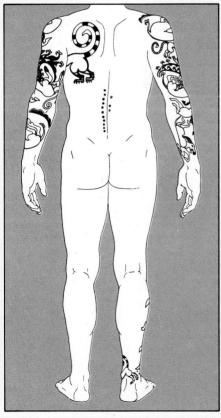

tract the brains from the skulls. The women were buried with their braids, and in the case of some of the men, false beards were provided.

The corpses lay in hollowed-out larchwood coffins, the sides of which were decorated with animal carvings or designs cut from pieces of leather or birchbark and applied to the wood. Sometimes a man and woman were buried together, placed foot to foot in a single long coffin. The clothes of the dead lay on top of the bodies, and some men had their right hands stitched to their pubic areas—a ritual the significance of which eludes the archeologists.

The peace of these carefully prepared dead apparently did not last long. Before the tombs filled with ice, the robbers entered through holes cut in the log roofing. And so thoroughly did they go about their business that when Rudenko himself entered the graves many centuries later he found that the plunderers had "left merely scraps" to provide only the most tantalizing glimpses of the treasure that once must have been strewn about the graves.

In their search for riches the robbers had callously disturbed the dead, severing the heads, arms and feet to remove necklaces and other ornaments, and tossing aside clothes. They even tore down colorful felt hangings on the log walls, perhaps in hope of finding hidden caches of gold.

Even so, Rudenko was not to be disappointed. Here —preserved for thousands of years in deep freeze— were articles made of wood, fabric, fur and leather, things that would have perished in ordinary graves but that miraculously survived to shed intimate light on the Altai horsemen.

Garments that were intact showed how they dressed. They preferred clothing of leather, fur or

Out of a frozen tomb in the Altai Mountains came the corpse of a woman who was 40 when she died 2,400 years ago. To embalm her, the brain was removed and the body eviscerated. Then balsam and herbs were inserted; the cavities were filled with horsehair and moss and closed with coarse stitches.

felt, although some of the men's shirts were woven of a hemplike fiber. Caftans for both men and women consisted of numerous pieces of chamois-like leather sewn together and sometimes ornamented with fanciful leather appliqués. Among other items of male attire were long stockings of heavy black or white felt with sewn-on felt soles, tunics with decorated sleeves, and peaked felt hats that matched a description in Herodotus of headgear worn by the Black Sea Scythians. The women had similar felt stockings; one had leopard fur boots whose soles were embroidered with beaded designs: when she sat cross-legged on the ground, she could show off the fancy soles.

Even more decorative than boots and clothing were the felt wall hangings. Brightly dyed in reds, blues, yellows and greens and often appliquéd with animal figures, they no doubt closely resembled hangings that had adorned the tents of the living—and may well have been taken from the tents occupied in life by the deceased. Among other possible household items were felt mats and rugs, one of them a pile carpet of Persian type more than six feet square and ornamented with plant designs, stars, griffins and a procession of men on horseback (page 134). This well-preserved carpet and another that Rudenko discovered some time later in a tomb a hundred miles or so away from the Pazyryk group are the earliest-known woolen pile rugs found anywhere.

Tossed about by the robbers were dozens of other objects that provided fascinating glimpses into the lives of the Altai horsemen. There was the collapsed ruin of a wooden ceremonial carriage with four multispoked wheels (page 57); there were small oval-topped tables whose legs could be removed for easy transportation, low stools, and a felt pillow stuffed with deer hair. There were also numerous leather pouches of different shapes and sizes. One small pouch contained a black dye; another held coriander seeds (Coriandrum sativum), apparently valued by the horsemen both as an antiseptic and as an aromatic. Silk purses and fabrics pointed to trade connections with China. A drum made of horn, a harplike stringed instrument and several mirrors suggested unexpected refinements in the nomads' culture. And in one tomb Rudenko came upon evidence that the Altai tribesmen, like their Black Sea brethren, inhaled hemp vapors. The evidence consisted not only of the poles and leather coverings for a hemp tent, but also of the receptacle containing the actual hemp seeds (page 106).

Rudenko was astonished by the remarkably high level of imagination and craftsmanship of various items—including the tombs themselves, whose logs had been cut and marked beforehand to guide the builder when they were assembled later. The collapsible tables reflected the practical concern of people often on the move. The clothing demonstrated sewing skills that even modern tailors would rate as superb. One large woven shirt was styled in four pieces—two for the front and two for the back—joined without gusseting and stitched together with fine red woolen braid and cord. The hem of one caftan displayed as many as 50 tiny stitches to an inch.

Only the separate graves of horses had escaped pilfering, and they provided Rudenko with the gaudiest proof of the Altai nomads' artistry. Ranging from small ordinary mounts to well-bred, powerful steeds—mostly chestnut and bay in color with a golden tint—the horses still wore simple saddles, saddlecloths, bridles and mane covers of felt and leather.

Such accouterments were often embellished with animal forms, some made of metal but most fashioned from leather and felt in bright reds, greens and blues. Leather and wood pendants, the latter occasionally faced with gold, festooned some of the riding gear. Several horses had been outfitted with strange mask-like decorations (page 54) of leather-covered felt that fitted over their heads like sheaths. These were embellished with animal motifs of many different kinds. One displayed on the front a blue appliquéd tiger adorned with small gold disks, and sprouting from its top was an almost life-sized pair of leather deer antlers, whose tines were tipped with tufts of red-dyed horsehair. On another head covering, a griffin, rising like a crest between the horse's ears, battled to the death with a feline whose contorted shape covered the horse's muzzle.

Removing such varied mementos from the ice must have been an eerie experience, and all the more so when the archeologists paused to think that these dead had probably grazed their herds on this very steppe region, that they had responded to the slow roll of the seasons, loved the sun and retreated from the cold. In winter they very likely repaired to encampments of sturdy log huts, as reflected perhaps in the very structure of their burial chambers. And when at last life had fled, they took their final refuge in the sheltered valleys.

Enriching though the Altai finds have been, they do not begin to answer all the many questions about the first horsemen, or even about this one particular group. Scholars still debate, for example, the origins of the Altai nomads, as they do those of the rulers of ancient Scythia. But the central question has been indisputably answered: though Herodotus' original chronicle seemed extravagant, as a matter of archeological fact the riders of the steppes did live and die much as the Father of History reported.

The Scythians' Extravagant Rites of Death

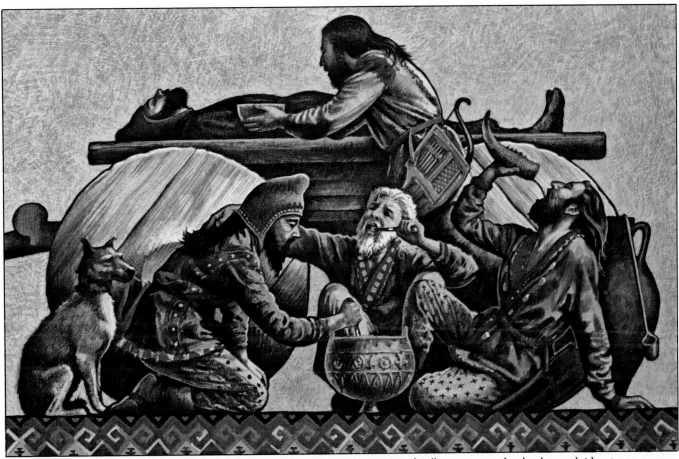

Three Scythians drown their sorrow in drinks of wine (foreground) as a fourth offers a cup to the dead man, laid out on a wagon.

Prolonged and demonstrative grieving followed the death of every Scythian tribesman. Forty days of processionals and ceremonial feasting were the standard prelude to laying a body in the grave. But such effusive expressions of sorrow were just a small part of the year-long series of rituals that followed the passing of a king. In tribute to the lost leader, members of every tribe in his domain joined the solemn march to the burial site, and once they arrived there they participated in prescribed rites of mourning, sacrifice and purification.

Fascinated by what seemed to him to be extraordinary death ceremonies, the tireless Greek chronicler Herodotus devoted as much care to describing the Scythians' way of death as he did to their way of life. Herodotus' detailed accounts, and recent archeological evidence that supports and expands them, provided the basis for the paintings on this and the following pages, and excerpts from his text accompany the illustrations.

Lacerations to Honor a Chief

When a Scythian king died, some of his subjects immediately set to work preparing an appropriate grave; others, in the meantime, readied his body for interment. Herodotus' description of the embalming process leaves very little to the imagination:

"They take the king's corpse and, having opened the belly and cleaned out the inside, fill it with a preparation of chopped cypress, frankincense, parsley seed, and aniseed, after which they sew up the opening, enclose the body in wax and, placing it on a wagon, carry it through all the different tribes *(above right)*.

"On this procession, each tribe, when it receives the corpse, imitates the example which is first set by the Royal Scythians; every man chops off a piece of his ear, crops his hair close, and makes a cut all around his arm, lacerates his forehead and his nose, and thrusts an arrow through his left hand *(below right)*. Then they who have care of the corpse carry it with them to another of the tribes which are under the Scythian rule, followed by those whom they first visited."

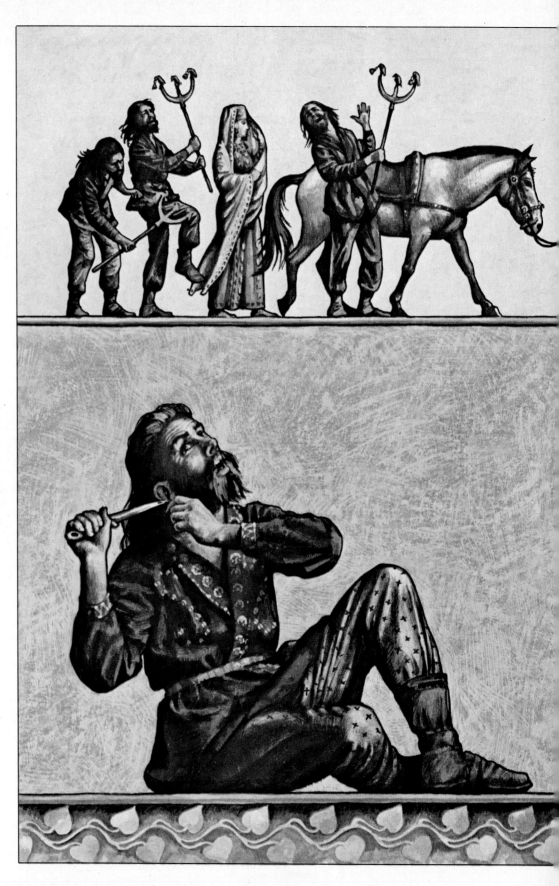

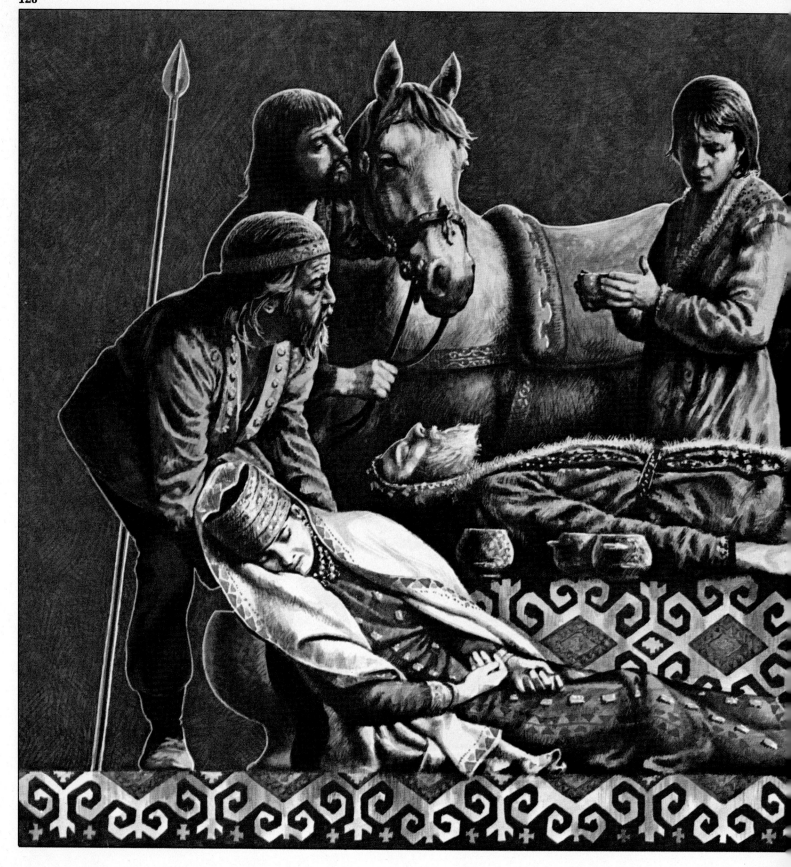

Readying a Retinue for the Afterlife

Herodotus never actually witnessed the burial of a king, but judging from evidence that has been discovered in tombs, his research was remarkably accurate. Although he could not have explored the interiors of the royal tombs, Herodotus knew that they were situated in a remote part of the steppe and that the tombs were "square in shape and of great size." He also knew that many of the companions who surrounded a king in life accompanied him in death.

When the mourners ended their funeral procession, wrote Herodotus, "they come to the tombs of the kings. There the body of the dead king is laid in the grave prepared for it, stretched upon a mattress; spears are fixed in the ground on either side of the corpse and beams stretched across above it to form a roof, which is covered with a thatching of twigs. In the open space around the king they bury one of his concubines *(bottom left)*, first killing her by strangling, and also his cupbearer, his cook, his groom, his lackey, his messenger, his horses, firstlings of all his other possessions and some golden cups—for they use neither silver nor brass. After this they set to work and raise a vast mound above the grave, all of them vying with each other and seeking to make it as tall as possible."

Ritual Purification and Intoxication

The ceremonies did not end when the ground was closed over a coffin. According to Herodotus, the next phase of the Scythians' mourning was a very curious rite, which he identified as a kind of cleansing:

"After the burial, those engaged in it purify themselves. First they wash their heads *(top left)*; their women make a combination of cypress, cedar and frankincense wood, which they pound into a paste. With this substance, they plaster their faces all over, and indeed their whole bodies *(top right)*. A sweet odor is imparted to them, and when they remove the plaster, their skin is clean and glossy.

"In order to cleanse their bodies, the men make a booth by fixing in the ground three sticks inclined toward one another, and stretching around them woolen felts; inside the booth a dish is placed on the ground, into which they put a number of red-hot stones, and then add some hemp seed. Hemp is very like flax; only that it is a much coarser and taller plant. The Scythians take some hemp seed, and creeping under the felt, throw it upon the red-hot stones. Immediately it gives out such a vapor as no Greek vapor bath can exceed; the Scyths shout for joy, and this vapor serves them instead of a water bath; for they never by any chance wash their bodies with water."

Herodotus made an understandable mistake in concluding that the hemp rites were comparable to the Greeks' vapor baths, but because the Scythians used no water, the tent could not have filled with cleansing steam. The intoxicating smoke was undoubtedly meant to transform the mind rather than to purify the body.

A Year Later, More Sacrifices

Mourning for a Scythian king, according to Herodotus, ended with a ceremony on the first anniversary of the king's death. Herodotus' account concludes with a description of the very last and most macabre rituals:

"When a year is gone by, further ceremonies take place. Fifty of the best of the late king's attendants are taken and are strangled, along with fifty of the most beautiful horses.

"When they are dead, their bowels are taken out, and the cavity is cleaned, filled full of chaff, and straightaway sewn up again. This done, a number of posts are set into the ground, in sets of two pairs each; atop every pair of stakes half the rim of a wheel is placed to form an arch. Then strong stakes are run lengthwise through the bodies of the horses from tail to neck, and they are set on top of the rims so that the arch in front supports the shoulders of the horse, while the one behind holds up the belly and quarters, the legs dangling in mid-air. Each horse is given a bit and bridle, which is later stretched out in front of the horse and fastened to a peg.

"The fifty strangled youths are then mounted on the fifty horses. To effect this, a stake is passed through their bodies along the course of the spine to the neck, the lower end of which projects from the body and is fixed into a socket made in the stake that runs lengthwise down the horse. The fifty riders are thus ranged in a circle round the tomb and so left."

Chapter Five: A Fierce, Free Heritage

"What sort of men are these?" That question must have perplexed the Persian leader Darius when, in the midst of battle, he watched his Scythian enemies abandon the serious business of war in order to take off suddenly in chase of a hare they had spied. The same query persists in the minds of modern civilized men as scholarship adds to what we know about the strange customs of Eurasia's mounted nomads, and as we remember that their barbaric heirs were the Huns and the Mongols, and that the latter forged a single confederacy of horse-borne tribes that caused all the known world to quake—and much of it to crumble—in the 13th Century A.D.

Clearly the term "civilized" wears a cloak of smugness; and the word "barbaric" carries a heavy pejorative cargo. With the notable exception of Herodotus, most ancient writers who observed the first horsemen tended to see them as oddities who did not quite fit within the spectrum of normal humanity. One Chinese court official said of the Hsiung-nu, who badgered and terrorized the border settlements of his homeland after the end of the Third Century B.C.: "In their breasts beat the hearts of beasts . . . from the most ancient times they have not been regarded as part of humanity."

How accurate were such judgments? Were they fair? Were the Scythians, the Sarmatians, the Hsiung-nu and, centuries later, the Huns and the Mongols really less rational than other peoples? How much

weight should be given to the most brutal aspects of their behavior?

When the Scythians swore an oath, Herodotus reported, they drank drops of each other's blood mixed with wine (page 98). Civilized men do not do this; the prospect seems hardly less odious than eating another human's flesh. It was the Scythians' custom, too, to take scalps and flaunt their enemies' skulls in order to humiliate their foes, confirm their kills and prove their prowess. It is also true that many horse-borne tribes made savage raids and merciless extortion routine practices.

But to acknowledge only such things is to fail in understanding these mounted nomads. It is also essential to appreciate that, by definition, nomadic peoples put little store in political boundaries; to realize that laws other than tribal conventions meant even less; to perceive that although they were often wild, they were also free.

The nomads' view of themselves and of their world emerges vividly from the uses to which the Scythians put gold—and its meaning to them. Like any other people with access to this treasured metal, the Scythians had it fashioned into beautiful objects. What made them unusual in this regard was their unstinting use of it. In the eyes of the conservative Greeks, the Scythians must have seemed profligate indeed. But the Scythians were extravagant in everything, at least in everything that the nomadic life allowed. Houses, monuments, temples and gardens —all the things on which settled peoples lavish their artistic attentions—were not part of the nomads' life. The horsemen could do little more than decorate their tents, their mounts and their own bodies.

In the shade of a tree, a Mongol warrior prepares to braid the tail of his sleek mount. Though a fine, well-groomed horse was the most treasured possession of a Mongol, he set great store as well by his own appearance. In this 15th Century painting on silk, the warrior's costume includes a gold helmet trimmed with fur, a brocade tunic and a gold-encrusted belt.

But beyond an obvious appeal to the eye and high economic value, gold held a special, spiritual significance for the Scythians. According to Herodotus, the Scythians associated the precious substance with their presence on earth, tracing the lineage of their supreme ruler to a miracle in bygone times when four golden objects fell from heaven. Thus the Scythians literally revered their gold. For this reason, explained Herodotus, "the Royal Scythians guard the sacred gold with the most special care, and year by year offer great sacrifices to its honor. . . . If the man who has custody of the gold should fall asleep . . . he is sure not to outlive the year."

Because of the divine aura of gold, the Scythians often employed it for artifacts with magical meanings and uses. Almost all their art, and that of the other steppe nomads as well, reflects a supernatural realm as populous with wild animals as was the real world of the grasslands. To the nomads, as to all other peoples who live close to nature, animals were more than just dumb creatures: they were manifestations of unseen forces, executors of the will of supernatural powers, bearers of cosmic messages.

It is not hard to understand how the beasts of the world came to possess such tremendous importance. Imagine the loneliness of a night on the endless expanse of the steppes. A gentle breeze ruffles the sea of grass. Stars, and perhaps a sliver of moon, cast a pale light on the camp. A pony snorts softly and shifts its weight from one hind foot to the other in its semisleep. Then an animal's shriek, sharp, high and cruel, shatters the calm. Characterizing the sudden, brief sound is as impossible as locating its source. Now everyone is awake, pulses racing, eyes alert but unseeing. Imagination takes flight, filling in what the

Genghis Khan began as chieftain of a tribe of mounted nomads and became one of history's greatest and most ruthless conquerors. After he died in 1227 A.D., his Mongol empire stretched almost 5,000 miles, from the coast of China to the Danube River in Europe. This near-contemporary portrait is in the former Imperial Palace at Peking.

eyes cannot discern. Every sound takes on meaning. Is it a warning? An omen? A curse?

In the nomad's world, the only real dangers were natural ones. Expert horsemanship and marksmanship, and the ability to vanish from sight in a quarter hour's time, equipped the nomad to handle his human enemies with relative ease. But he and his domesticated herds were at the mercy of fire, weather, disease and predatory animals. The nomad believed that invisible spirits—some benevolent, most capable of sudden violence and all possessed of strong will—controlled these forces and determined the tribe's physical welfare. Untamed animals, also willful and uncontrollable, belonged partly to this supernatural realm; in their mercurial behavior, they seemed to move with the energy of the spirits, their curious cries expressing deep meanings.

In fact, in the nomad's view of things, there were times when spirits cloaked in animal disguises mingled with people. Thus animals could act as intermediaries between the supernatural and natural worlds, bearing messages and carrying out wishes.

The nomad believed that the spirits could be influenced and even manipulated, but only by a specialist. In nomadic societies, and among some settled peoples as well, that specialist was the shaman. Part medium, part fortuneteller, part medicine man, a shaman dealt with all problems that were beyond the resources of ordinary tribesmen. He went wherever his tribe went, but lived a life quite apart; in effect, he was a portable cathedral, a one-man priesthood, a diagnostician and a curer of all ills.

Animals, whether real or rendered in artifacts, protected the powers of a shaman's soul, and they were his assistants in conversing with the supernatural. In fact, a shaman's soul was believed to reside partly inside some beast—usually a wild one such as a wolf, an eagle or a bear—and thus the shaman was actually thought to be part animal. The nomads believed, therefore, that any wilderness creature might be a holy man in his nonhuman form.

The shaman spoke to the forces of nature in animal utterances, often in nighttime seances amid total darkness. Usually he was in a trance, achieved sometimes with the help of a hallucinogen such as hemp, but more frequently merely by the effort of his own highly trained will. While in such a spell, it was believed, he acquired the wisdom of the universe, which enabled him to interpret signs, see forward in time and perform miracles of healing.

The shaman's visions might have inspired the patterns and themes in the steppe nomads' art: the whorls and zigzags, composite creatures, dismembered limbs and floating features—all seem to be hallucinations transformed into reality.

Only one other member of the tribal society held a comparably honored position: the metalsmith. He may have been the only other mortal privy to some of the shaman's secrets. In some societies, one man might have served the dual function of both shaman and smith. Like the shaman, the smith was regarded as something of a sorcerer because he wielded fire. He could make dull materials become incandescent; in his hands, solids turned to liquid and then, after hardening again, they assumed the forms of writhing, glittering creatures.

Had the first mounted nomads left nothing more to posterity than their Animal Style art, the development of horsemanship and the graves in which they buried their dead, their place in history might be little more than an interesting footnote. But the nomads' legacy consisted of much more. The earliest horsemen created a way of life, and it outlasted the Scythians, the Sarmatians and the Hsiung-nu alike.

Of all the places where the first horsemen's way of life survived, eastern Asia saw it take its most ferocious form. The Hsiung-nu began a long tradition of brutality. By the Second Century B.C., these horsemen were incorporating most of Mongolia into an empire whose strength rivaled the might of the highly centralized bureaucracy of neighboring China. For the Hsiung-nu, China was a limitless mine of wealth to be exploited by any means—but especially by extortion. If threats failed to produce the goods and treasure that the nomads desired, they retaliated not with a few murders but with rampages that razed whole provinces.

And they reinforced their military strength with shrewd trading tactics. One of the major commodities the Chinese got in trade from the Hsiung-nu was horses—the motive power of the Chinese army. Thus the Hsiung-nu could influence the very ability of China to combat them; should the horsemen choose to hobble the Chinese militia, they could simply curtail its supply of horses.

Through such means, the Hsiung-nu tribes were able to annoy and frustrate the Chinese. But why did they bother? What did they need from the industrious people of China? Not being farmers themselves, they had to have food, and the agricultural abundance of China supplied them with grains and livestock aplenty. They needed iron as well, and this the Chinese also supplied. But they also craved silk—for its dazzling colors, for its luxurious texture. Silk was more beautiful and more prestigious than anything that could be made from materials available on the steppes. Living in the dry, windy landscape of Mongolia, the Hsiung-nu desired extravagantly beautiful things that they could drape over their bodies while they rode, or sat cross-legged inside their yurts.

At least one Chinese city dweller, a court official obliged to travel in the retinue of a Chinese princess betrothed to a Hsiung-nu ruler, made it his business to warn the Hsiung-nu of the pitfalls of luxury. "Your whole horde," the courtier advised his hosts, "scarcely equals the population of a couple of Chinese prefectures, but the secret of your strength lies in your independence of China for all your real necessities. I notice an increasing fondness for Chinese luxuries. Reflect that one-fifth of the Chinese wealth would suffice to buy your people completely. Silks and satins are not half so well suited as felts to the rough life you lead, nor are the perishable delicacies of China so handy as your kumiss and cheese."

The courtier clearly admired the nomads for what they were: natural aristocrats who answered to no masters but themselves. Nonetheless, he owed his primary allegiance to his own people. Aware that the Hsiung-nu's arrogance was growing, he suspected that the nomads were not to be trusted. He advised the Chinese court that they must be ever on guard lest they invite the riders' murderous wrath.

The courtier's worst expectations turned out to be correct. In the Fifth Century A.D., another band of nomads—the Huns—swarmed out of Central Asia. Their leader, Attila, aspired to bring all Asia and Europe under his sole dominion. Wherever they rode, the Huns raised havoc and collected bounty. In 451 A.D., Attila's forces took on the greatest power in

Text continued on page 135

A Rich Cache of Rare Textiles from Distant Lands

Elegant and elaborately worked textiles—examples are the embroidered silk shabrack, or saddlecloth, at right and the sheared-wool-pile rug on page 134—were found in 1949 in the frozen Pazyryk burial mounds by Soviet archeologist S. I. Rudenko. Discovered solidly encased in ice that had preserved them for more than 2,300 years, the silk and wool fibers are among the oldest remains of their kind —but still retain their color.

Even more remarkable than their survival are the facts of their origin. The shabrack traveled from China to the Altai Mountains and the rug probably from Persia, about 2,000 miles away. Both doubtless came into the hands of Altai tribesmen through trade, in exchange for gold or furs or even a well-bred riding horse.

In the same barrow as the imported textiles, Rudenko found a singular example of local art—a felt appliqué windscreen *(overleaf)*. With poles to support it, the screen could be erected in front of a dwelling to protect the entrance from fierce mountain winds.

A stylized pheasant standing on a flowering branch is one of many birds delicately embroidered on a silk shabrack found at Pazyryk. The fabric, of which only a detail is shown, was probably woven to celebrate the marriage of a wealthy Chinese woman. But the Altai tribesmen who took it in trade added horsehair tassels to one end and used it as a saddlecloth.

Stuffed with fine deer hair, three-dimensional felt swans like this one from a tomb at Pazyryk are thought to be decorations for a large canopy that covered the top of a burial carriage.

A repeating pattern of a strangely masculine goddess facing a horseman adorns a 21-foot-long windscreen found at Pazyryk, of which this piece is a small section. The horseman rides without stirrups and carries a gorytus, or bow-and-arrow case, on his left hip. The felt figures are appliquéd on sheep's wool. The bodies of bald women have been found in the burial mounds, but the portrayal of a goddess with a hat and no hair suggests that living women also shaved their heads.

In a detail from a six- by six-and-one-half-foot rug, the central field is enclosed by borders of fallow deer and griffins. The stars that fill the center are repeated, with the colors reversed, to separate the grazing deer and mounted horsemen, like the one shown below. The fine articulation of the figures is due to the density of the pile; there are 215 knots per square inch, which means the rug probably took about 18 months to make.

The rug's outer edge, a wide band not seen in the detail at right, includes men on horses, moving in a counterclockwise direction. The sturdy horse, with its knotted tail, proudly arches its neck as if to show off the plume on top of its head. The rider—dressed in what may be Persian attire, with a hood that ties under his chin—sits on a fringed shabrack.

the West—the Roman Empire. But death cut short Attila's conquests. It was not until 800 years later that his imperial dream would be made a reality, by another Asian horseman—the Mongol autocrat known as Genghis Khan.

In the 13th Century A.D., after consolidation by Genghis Khan and his descendants, the Mongol empire stretched from the Pacific coast to the Danube River. Its northernmost frontier was the Siberian pine forests, and its southern boundary was formed by the impenetrable peaks of the Himalayas.

The Mongols' homeland was exactly the same terrain where the Hsiung-nu had roamed more than a millennium before. But the exact origins of the Mongols are obscure; no one can say for certain where they lived before they became a conspicuous force in Mongolia, and no one knows who their cultural ancestors were. Except for their beginnings, however, the Mongols' story is anything but mysterious. Although they had no written language, their leaders hired literate foreigners to record their achievements. In addition, their exploits were chronicled by numerous writers in both the East and the West, who assembled one of the best-documented chapters in history. Strikingly, the descriptions of the Mongols' way of life correspond in almost every detail—dress, diet, customs, pursuits—to those of their nomadic predecessors and successors (pages 143-153).

The Mongols' own mythology furnished several accounts of their beginnings, though none is very helpful to scholars. One legend held that they sprang from a blue wolf. Another, only slightly less fanciful, traced the Mongols back to a widow's miraculous conception, which produced their earliest ancestor, a

heroic figure by the name of Budantsar. According to this story, seven generations intervened between Budantsar and the leader who singlehandedly was to build their empire: a boy who at birth was named Temuchin and who, when he reached middle age, prophetically conferred upon himself the name Genghis Khan, signifying mighty emperor.

Mongol lore held that Temuchin came into the world clutching in his tiny fist a clot of blood that was as hard and luminous as a ruby. To the tribe's holy men this was a sign that Temuchin was destined to become a terrible tyrant. The boy showed the promise of military prowess early in life. By the age of 11, it was said, he could ride and shoot with bow and arrow as well as any grown man.

The holy men's prediction proved correct. Temuchin devoted his early manhood to the task of unifying the numerous disparate tribes of Mongolia and to bringing them all together under his control. One by one, prominent nomad warriors pledged allegiance to Temuchin; those who did not either took flight or perished.

At last, in 1206, when Temuchin had already reached middle age and his position as leader of all the Mongolian nomads was secure, he was proclaimed Genghis Khan. All the lesser chieftains of the diverse tribes under him acquiesced to his leadership and recognized him as their supreme ruler. On a riverbank in the heart of Genghis Khan's territory a standard was erected—a tall wooden pole with the tails of nine yaks affixed to its top. This symbol of might was to accompany the Great Khan in every campaign from that time forward.

Then the new emperor set about organizing a proper army. In effect, the entire Mongol nation was to be

one vast cavalry; the women would serve as defense while the men took the offense. The entire force might not go into action at once, but all its parts were prepared to fight with terrific speed and precision.

The impeccable coordination essential to make this scheme work was achieved by following the standard organization of a nomad army and honing its effectiveness. The largest unit consisted of 10,000 men; it, in turn was divided into groups of 1,000; the units of 1,000 were organized into groups of 100; and each of these into units of 10. Officers commanded at every level, but the Khan did not neglect the old tribal loyalties that his soldiers still kept from the days before their unification. He selected his officers with care, seeing to it that units were led by commanders held in high regard. Still, he might reject a leader with greater stamina in favor of one with less, to assure that no officer would push his men harder than they were physically capable of going.

Discipline was rigid, and punishments were harsh.

The death penalty was imposed for insubordination, but also for showing undue kindness to a captive, for harboring a runaway slave, for falling asleep on guard duty, for stepping unbidden over the threshold of a commanding officer's tent. An officer could be executed for seeking special favors from anybody except the Khan himself.

With the Great Khan's ascension there came the first code of laws that the Mongolian nomads had ever known. Because the Khan was illiterate, he dictated his code to a scribe who was proficient in one of the written languages of Central Asia.

Called the Great Yasa, the laws included many customs that had been traditional in the region. The Yasa forbade deceitfulness, treachery, theft and adultery. It advocated respect for the learned and wise and mercy for the innocent, the aged and the poor. For such crimes as commercial fraud and bankruptcy, the Yasa prescribed capital punishment, as it also did for such offenses as contaminating running water by

At a Mongol camp, as horses graze and underfed dogs play (bottom, left and center), two nomads (top left) wash their clothes, another nurtures the fire and a fourth (lower right) leans on his saddle, conversing with a slave. The equipment (top right) includes a sword, bow, quiver and water jugs. The painting dates from the 14th Century A.D.

bathing in it, or for urinating into a hearth, a stream or inside a yurt. Lesser violations were penalized by heavy fines or beatings.

Enforcement of the Yasa was strict and direct; the Khan made sure he knew what was going on in every corner of his realm. For this purpose he retained a personal guard—the finest soldiers in the land —picked from the ranks of the regular army. The members of this special force, which gradually grew to number 10,000 men, personally bore all news to the Khan. They were in touch with literally all Mongols, and so in turn was their supreme ruler. For the mounted nomads, who had habitually attended to their own intratribal affairs, this was the first time the will of one man affected them all.

Within a year of his ascension, Genghis Khan was ready to expand his hegemony. His horde was in fine condition. One hundred and twenty thousand Mongols stood ready to fight, each man carrying food supplies, weapons and armor—including a quiver of arrows and a short bow, a spear, a shield and a dagger. Every soldier had an iron helmet and a coat of scale armor that protected him from the throat to just above the knees.

And there were mounts aplenty, as many as six or seven spares per soldier—rugged ponies that stood only 14 hands high. Raised by the tens of thousands in the pastures of northern Mongolia, these little horses needed to be watered only once a day; on the move, they thrived on little more than whatever grass was available. Still, the Mongols understood their value and cherished them; the rule was that no horse could be ridden more often than one day in four.

To the west of the Khan's Mongolian stronghold lay territory held by four bands of nomads; to the south was the rival kingdom of Si-Hsia. The Khan coveted these lands, comprising some 230,000 square miles, as well as their huge population—potential recruits for the Mongol army. A series of swift, decisive campaigns brought all the neighboring nomads under control, and in 1210 the Si-Hsia succumbed when the Khan's army besieged Egrigaia, their capital city.

The Khan, now with nothing to fear from his flanks, was ready to take northern China. The assault was not to be a quick triumph however. Six years of scouting and espionage, of advances and retreats, of patient waits through burning summers, of treaty offers and refusals went by. But the Khan's strategy was perfect. The Mongols swarmed across the Gobi Desert. Some of them swung around to the northwest of Chung-tu, the capital of the Chin emperors, where modern Peking now stands. Others swept down the Korean peninsula. Their enemies died by the thousands, their rotting bodies raising a stench that was to become familiar throughout Asia and half of Europe. A trail of smoke from burning towns always remained in the wake of the Khan's army. The final blow was the siege of Chung-tu; hunger and an epidemic of plague forced open the city's gates and looting, murderous Mongol hordes flooded in.

In 1215, the Khan contemplated the advantages of a trade treaty with one of Central Asia's reigning powers: Muhammad, ruler of the huge Khwarazmian Empire, east of the Caspian Sea. A fanatical proponent of the Islamic faith, whose leaders were engaged in a vigorous drive for converts, Muhammad was well informed about Genghis Khan's exploits in China, and he thought an alliance with him would be an auspicious diplomatic move.

Clad in coats of iron mail, Mongol cavalrymen pursue their adversaries with drawn sabers in an illustration from a 14th Century A.D. manuscript. Despite a reputation for battlefield ferocity, the Mongols managed to avoid hand-to-hand combat by resorting to ruses that took their enemies unaware.

The Khan received Muhammad's emissaries with grace. He returned word to Muhammad that such an arrangement would please him—so much so, in fact, that he would accord Muhammad the status of "dearest of his sons." The Muslim potentate was outraged; the terms were clearly intended to put him in the position of a vassal. To Muhammad the only answer to such an insult was war.

Three hundred thousand men mustered behind Muhammad; only half as many rallied to the generals in command of Genghis Khan's forces. But the Mongols came to battle with the newly acquired advantages of the most ingenious Chinese technology: short-range flame throwers and artillery—catapults, ballistae and even cannons. The ballistae, heavy siege catapults, could hurl projectiles weighing 300 pounds each. Under their armor, the Mongols wore another Chinese invention: shirts of heavy silk that could not easily be pierced by arrows. If an arrow struck the silk, the fabric would enter the wound

still covering the arrowhead, allowing a wounded man to remove the missile from his flesh with a minimum of pain and loss of blood.

The Khan's army campaigned against the Muslims for four years and at the end of that time had advanced westward another 2,000 miles, annexing most of western Asia to Genghis Khan's domain. History affords one index to the terror: in just four cities, five million citizens were reported dead. And the conquest of Russia and eastern Europe was yet to come.

But Genghis Khan's aspirations outlasted his body. He died in 1227, after successfully suppressing a rebellion north of the Chinese border. He breathed his last lying in a felt yurt similar to the tent he had been born in, and his body was carried back to Mongolia. Although he himself never entered Europe, the conquest and destruction continued after Genghis Khan's death. His successors were to wreak havoc in Russia, Poland and Hungary.

To survive a Mongol invasion was to live for revolt

—or at least to try. The nomad conquerors were well aware of this and so they resorted to mass slaughter. Batu Khan, one of Genghis Khan's grandsons and ruler of what in Russia came to be called the Golden Horde, was one of the most thorough, and sadistic, murderers in history.

A 20th Century scholar, Sir Robert Kennaway Douglas, writing nearly seven centuries after Batu Khan's invasion of Russia, compiled a heart-rending account based on contemporary observations. "With irresistible vigor and astonishing speed," Sir Robert wrote, "the Mongols made their way through the forests of Penza and Tambov, and appeared before the beautiful city of Ryazan. For five days they discharged a ceaseless storm of shot from their ballistae and, having made a breach in the defenses, carried the city by assault on the twenty-first of December, 1237. The prince, with his mother, wife [and] sons, the boyars and the inhabitants, without regard to age or sex, were slaughtered with the savage cruelty of Mongol revenge; some were impaled, some shot at with arrows for sport, others were flayed or had nails or splinters of wood driven under their nails. Priests were roasted alive, and nuns and maidens ravished in the churches before their relatives. No eye remained open to weep for the dead."

Meanwhile, the Mongols' leaders were developing a taste for the luxury and elegance that only a sedentary life affords. Despite the time-honored nomad tradition of transience and mobility, a Mongol capital town was growing up in the south of Mongolia. Called Karakorum, it had begun to be something of an administrative and commercial center during Genghis Khan's regime.

During the reign of Ogodei, Genghis Khan's third son, Karakorum became a true city, with temples, marketplaces, government buildings and a palace set in a great, walled courtyard. According to eyewitness accounts, the palace was splendid to behold. It was constructed like a cathedral, with a long nave

A fanged demon, perhaps representing some force of nature, carries off a horse in another 14th Century A.D. Mongol drawing.

separated from side aisles by colonnades. When the khans held audiences, they sat enthroned on a high dais at the nave's northern end.

There in 1254 Mongke Khan, Ogodei Khan's nephew, received a traveler from France named William of Rubruck. Of all the sights at the royal court, what struck Rubruck most deeply was a fabulous fountain that spewed forth torrents of four delectable drinks. "In front of the throne," wrote Rubruck, "was placed a silver tree, having at its base four lions, from whose mouths there spouted into four silver basins wine, kumiss, hydromel [a honey drink] and terrasine [rice beer]. At the top of the tree a silver angel sounded a trumpet when the reservoirs that supplied the four fountains wanted replenishing."

The wonders of the Karakorum palace were nothing compared to the splendors that another grandson of Genghis Khan's, Kubilai, was to build in China. Kubilai Khan, a different kind of Mongol emperor, holds a special place in history. He is remembered as a benevolent, order-loving ruler who tolerated diverse religions and who hospitably received visitors from faraway places into his lavish realm. Nevertheless, he did not betray his lineage.

Born in 1214, he assumed power over the Mongols' northern Chinese dominions in 1260. As a general, he did the memory of his grandfather proud. His personal supremacy over all China was won during a 19-year span of wars: the first against a Mongol rival, and then against armies of the still unconquered Sung Empire south of the Yangtze River. By 1279, his hegemony reached as far south as Burma; he held nearly all the Pacific Coast; the western boundary of his Chinese domain was Tibet. His uncles, brothers and cousins, meanwhile, still ruled all the surrounding territory. But Kubilai was their ultimate leader—the Khan of all other khans.

The Chinese themselves recognized him as their legitimate emperor, proclaiming him the Son of Heaven, and his ascension marked the beginning of the Yuan Dynasty. The line was to last only 89 years—a brief span in Chinese terms—but under its aegis the fine arts of China flourished. The serene landscape paintings and the delicate, perfect porcelains produced by Chinese artists during the short, peaceful decades of the Yuan period remain in sharp contrast to the violence and savagery of an earlier time.

Kubilai made his winter capital on the site of the ancient city of Chung-tu—the city his grandfather had sacked some 60 years before—and he renamed it Tai-du: Great Capital. The marvels he had built there taxed the ability of stunned visitors to describe them. One chronicler, a Persian named Rashid-ed-Din, strained to convey the enormity of the palace's surrounding walls. The distance between them, he wrote, "is so great that an arrow shot with great force just carried across them." Nearby, Rashid continued, the Emperor had raised an artificial hillock on which he had planted "the most beautiful evergreen trees." These, Rashid said, were dug up from all parts of the empire and brought to Tai-du by elephants. The soil of which the little hill was made left a pit in the ground, which the Khan's workmen transformed into an ornamental pond that was stocked with swans and other water birds.

The Khan's summer palace was, if anything, even more glorious. Built at a place called Xandu, it was celebrated nearly five centuries later by the English poet Samuel Taylor Coleridge in his romantic work "Kubla Khan":

In Xanadu did Kubla Khan
A stately pleasure-dome decree:
Where Alph, the sacred river, ran
Through caverns measureless to man
  Down to a sunless sea.
So twice five miles of fertile ground
With walls and towers were girdled round:
And there were gardens bright with sinuous rills,
Where blossomed many an incense-bearing tree;
And here were forests ancient as the hills,
Enfolding sunny spots of greenery.

Coleridge's description, like his spelling of the ancient, alien names, was more poetic than literal, however. Certainly the most vivid account of Kubilai's "stately pleasure-dome" comes from the writings of Marco Polo. While on a trading mission far from his birthplace in Venice, Marco Polo found himself in the midst of the Mongols' Chinese empire, where he remained for 20 years. During his stay Marco undertook to inspect and chronicle nearly every aspect of the mighty Khan's realm. Little escaped the Venetian's keen and curious eye. He counted every man in the royal guard, noted every crop that grew in the surrounding countryside. From his precisely detailed description of Kubilai's summer palace, it might be possible to reconstruct it today.

In the middle of an enclosed park, as the diligent Italian set the scene, stood the palace "constructed entirely of canes, but with the interior all gilt and decorated with beasts and birds of very skillful workmanship. It is raised on gilt and varnished pillars, on each of which stands a dragon, entwining the pillar with its tail and supporting the roof on his outstretched limbs. The roof is made of canes, so well varnished that it is quite waterproof.

"Let me explain how it is constructed. You must know that these canes are more than three palms in girth and from ten to fifteen paces long. They are sliced down through the middle from one knot to the next, making two shingles. These canes are thick and long enough not only for roofing but for every sort of construction. The palace, then, is built entirely of such canes. As a protection against the wind each shingle is fastened with nails. And the Great Khan has had it designed so that it can be moved whenever he fancies; for it is held in place by more than 200 cords of silk."

Marco's observations were not limited merely to his physical surroundings. He also delved deeply into the Mongols' method of commerce and social customs, and he made special note of the numerous religious observances that dotted the calendar of the Mongols in China.

In Kubilai's court, he reported, the most important of all holy days was the springtime White Feast, celebrated on the 9th of May. On that day, the Khan's minions rounded up 10,000 mares and stallions, all pure white and revered as sacred. The horses were given shelter in the royal stables and had free, unimpeded run of the royal grounds.

Only the Khan himself, his family and a few specially selected persons were allowed to drink the milk from the white mares. Then, on the 28th of August, Kubilai Khan scattered to the winds great quantities of the white mares' milk as an offering to the divine spirits—a ceremony bearing testimony to the Mongols' roots in the prehistoric past, when horses first bore the Scythians, the Sarmatians and the Hsiung-nu to ascendancy over the Eurasian steppes.

A Centuries-old Way of Life

Nomadic horsemen, bundled up to insulate themselves against harsh winds and baking sun, prepare to set out across the steppe.

Right down to modern times, mounted nomads have roamed the Eurasian steppes, leading much the same kind of existence as the first horsemen of antiquity. Late in the 19th Century an itinerant Ukrainian photographer, Samuel M. Dudin, recorded their way of life. Traveling deep into Central Asia to a nomad encampment near Semipalatinsk in the eastern region of what is now the Soviet republic of Kazakhstan, Dudin exposed some 600 glass-plate negatives during the summer of 1899, most of which were purchased by the Ethnological Museum in Hamburg, Germany, and preserved there as a unique record.

The people Dudin photographed were Kazakhs, a Turkic name meaning riders of the steppes. At the time, they numbered several million, and their territory stretched almost 2,000 miles, from the lower Volga River in Russia to the borders of the Sinkiang region of China. Although they had been converted to the Muslim faith, the Kazakhs traced their earliest origins to the Turkic and Mongolian nomads who, under Genghis Khan and his descendants, galloped out of northern China to terrorize and dominate all of Asia and eastern Europe during the 13th Century.

Today, the Kazakhs are citizens of the Soviet Union, leading a settled life as farmers and stockbreeders. But when Dudin visited them, they were still wanderers, traveling hundreds of miles each year in search of fresh pastures for the great herds of sheep, goats, horses, camels and cattle on which their lives depended.

The folding sections of a yurt's walls, strapped together with thongs, are fitted with a door frame. Next, roof poles will be pegged into the crown and

A Portable Home on the Plains

The yurt, the Kazakh's portable dwelling, was a domed hut covered with heavy felt mats. Sturdily built to keep out cold and to withstand the winds sweeping the open steppe, the yurt consisted of a collapsible birch and willow framework to which a layer of reed screens and as many as 10 felts were tied. A yurt might be up to 20 feet in diameter. As many as 15 yurts, each housing a family, made up the typical camp, most members of which were related to the headman.

Easily transported by cart or pack animal, the yurt could be set up in an hour and taken down in half the time. Raising and dismantling the yurt was done by the women or the family's poor dependents. When in search of new campsites, the nomads each night might set up only the felt-covered dome structure or part of the wall to provide temporary shelter.

After ringing the yurt's frame with decorative willow-reed screens, a woman ties pieces of thick felt to the walls with woolen cords. During heat waves the felt could be rolled up or removed entirely. During cold spells a second layer of felt could be added.

the entire structure will be wrapped in felt mats. Carts very similar to the one seen here were used by the first horsemen for transporting belongings.

A wagonload of family possessions is ready to be moved into this completed yurt. The door, in this case a decorated felt curtain, was sometimes made of carved or painted wood. The flap on the roof could be pulled open to admit light or to allow the smoke of the hearth fire to escape, or it could be pulled shut to keep the rain out. Coated with grease, the felt covering the yurt shed rain and kept the tent watertight.

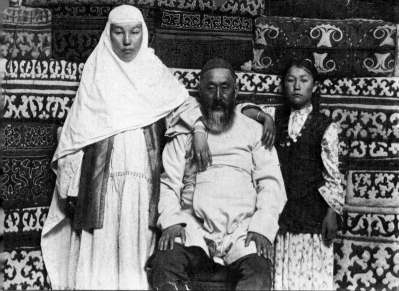

Stacks of chests covered with felt hold this family's possessions.

The Lavish Decor of a Yurt

The Kazakh's felt tent may have been all Spartan simplicity on the outside, but behind the door or the felt curtain (called the *ish kir mas,* "the dog shall not enter"), there was hardly an inch of space that was not covered by woven carpets, and rugs, hangings and mats of felt. The felts were lavishly embroidered or appliquéd with floral designs, animal motifs and arabesques. Long hours in the making, the decorative felts were designed by women called *aimochu,* "skilled ones," who improvised their own patterns based on traditional themes.

Within the yurt, all visitors were welcomed. They were led to the place of honor, offered meat or cheese and a jug of fermented mare's milk—kumiss. After that, and only then, did the talking begin, as the nomads, eager for news, plied their guests with a steady stream of questions.

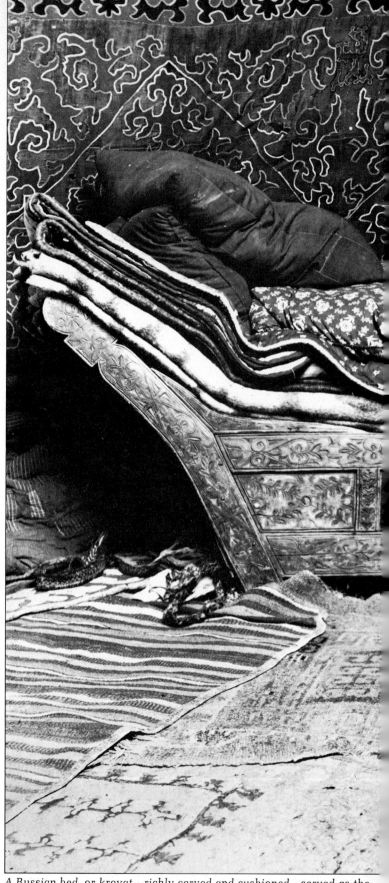

A Russian bed, or krovat—richly carved and cushioned—served as the

place of honor inside this snug yurt. No matter what its size and weight, the prized krovat, too, was transported on a cart from campsite to campsite.

A Kazakh woman tends a cradled infant.

Daily Occupations of Kazakh Women

Women did most of the work in the Kazakh camp. Wearing broad cotton headdresses—white if they were married, red if single—women cooked, made felt, sewed, wove, tended the children, milked the sheep and camels, fetched the water, collected dry sheep dung to fuel the hearth fire, saddled up their husbands' horses, raised the yurt at new campsites and took it down when the time came to move on.

Frequently, there was more than one wife in each household to share the burdens, in which case the newest wife got the hardest work until she bore her first child. But while their lives were difficult, Kazakh women had a voice, and their advice was sought and respected by their menfolk. Moreover, a woman was mistress of her yurt and often its owner as well, since a yurt usually formed a part of her dowry from her family.

Before serving kumiss, a woman stirs the fermented milk in a big leather sack.

Preparing felt for rugs and mats, women first beat wool to soften it. Next they will wet it with hot water, and then press and roll it between straw mats so that the fibers will mesh. Later they will unroll it, pound it for several hours, and dry it in the sun.

Seated at a ground loom, two women weave a wool binding for a yurt cover. Similar bands also served as saddle girths and decorative sashes.

During the foaling season Kazakh men fill wooden buckets with mare's milk, which will be made into kumiss, cheese and butter.

Varied Pursuits of Kazakh Men

During the warmer months, the true domain of Kazakh men, like that of the first horsemen, was not their camp but the open steppe. Tireless riders, the Kazakhs spent most of the day in the saddle: tending herds, scouting out new campsites, visiting neighboring camps to trade or inquire about grazing conditions. Even their favorite sports, racing and hunting, centered on horsemanship. Because the Kazakhs spent much of their lives on horseback, they wore clothes suited to riding, based on ancient prototypes: long padded coats and thick trousers of leather or felt. Only the high leather boots, with heels, were modern.

Around camp, the men did little. Metal- and woodworking were male occupations, but the men's most common domestic chores were milking the mares and, at night, guarding the animals that were kept beyond the camp.

A Kazakh silversmith fashions a buckle, while a young helper works the bellows.

A falcon, trained to hunt small game, sits on its master's arm. Among Kazakhs, as among some first horsemen, falconry was a popular sport.

Pushing and pulling on wooden handles to rotate the stone wheel, two boys help to grind grain—usually a woman's task.

Kazakhs and other tribes who rode the steppes gather for horse trading near Semipalatinsk, a city in eastern Kazakhstan. Observing traditions that

Rugged Cycle of the Nomads' Year

Except in winter, a time when severe cold and penetrating winds drove the Kazakhs into the sheltered, wooded river valleys, they were a people on the move *(right)*. They sometimes covered as much as 200 miles in a single year as they sought fresh pastures for their large herds.

In the summer, when the dried-out steppe offered little nourishment for their animals, the nomads scattered in small groups and migrated from spot to spot. Sometimes they went to the moist forest at the edge of the steppe, sometimes into the foothills of the Altai Mountains of Kazakhstan. Rarely did they stay more than a few days in one place. Living on the open steppe was easy only in spring and early autumn, when the rains brought relief, the grasslands provided food in abundance and the nomads were able to reassemble *(above)*.

Loaded with household gear, a family caravan makes its way to a new campsite. Two-humped

came down to them intact from their ancient ancestors, they celebrated such yearly get-togethers with races, games and displays of riding skills.

Bactrian camels, able to carry up to 600 pounds each, were the Kazakhs' primary beasts of burden. Horses were used almost exclusively for riding.

The Emergence of Man

This chart records the progression of life on earth from its first appearance in the warm waters of the new-formed planet through the evolution of man himself; it traces his physical, social, technological and intellectual development to the Christian era. To place these advances in commonly used chronological sequences, the column at the

Geology	Archeology	Billions of Years Ago	
Precambrian earliest era		4.5	Creation of the Earth
		4	Formation of the primordial sea
		3	First life, single-celled algae and bacteria, appears in water
		2	
		1	
		Millions of Years Ago	
			First oxygen-breathing animals appear
		800	
			Primitive organisms develop interdependent specialized cells
Paleozoic ancient life		600	Shell-bearing multicelled invertebrate animals appear
			Evolution of armored fish, first animals to possess backbones
		400	Small amphibians venture onto land
			Reptiles and insects arise
			Thecodont, ancestor of dinosaurs, arises
Mesozoic middle life		200	Age of dinosaurs begins
			Birds appear
			Mammals live in shadow of dinosaurs
			Age of dinosaurs ends
		80	
			Prosimians, earliest primates, develop in trees
Cenozoic recent life		60	
		40	Monkeys and apes evolve
		20	
		10	Ramapithecus, oldest known primate with apparently manlike traits, evolves in India and Africa
		8	
		6	Australopithecus, closest primate ancestor to man, appears in Africa
		4	

Geology	Archeology	Millions of Years Ago	
Lower Pleistocene oldest period of most recent epoch	**Lower Paleolithic** oldest period of Old Stone Age	2	Oldest known tool fashioned by man in Africa
		1	First true man, Homo erectus, emerges in East Indies and Africa
			Homo erectus populates temperate zones
		Thousands of Years Ago	
Middle Pleistocene middle period of most recent epoch		800	Man learns to control and use fire
		600	
			Large-scale, organized elephant hunts staged in Europe
		400	Man begins to make artificial shelters from branches
		200	
Upper Pleistocene latest period of most recent epoch	**Middle Paleolithic** middle period of Old Stone Age		Neanderthal man emerges in Europe
		80	
		60	Ritual burials in Europe and Near East suggest belief in afterlife
			Woolly mammoths hunted by Neanderthals in northern Europe
			Cave bear becomes focus of cult in Europe
		40	
	Upper Paleolithic latest period of Old Stone Age		Cro-Magnon man arises in Europe
			Asian hunters cross Bering Land Bridge to populate New World
			Oldest known written record, lunar notations on bone, made in Europe
			Man reaches Australia
			First artists decorate walls and ceilings of caves in France and Spain
		30	Figurines sculpted for nature worship
		20	Invention of needle makes sewing possible
			Bison hunting begins on Great Plains of North America
Holocene present epoch	**Mesolithic** Middle Stone Age	10	Bow and arrow invented in Europe
			Pottery first made in Japan

(vertical label between Upper Pleistocene columns: **Last Ice Age**)

▼ Four billion years ago   ▼ Three billion years ago

▲ Origin of the Earth (4.5 billion)   ▲ First life (3.5 billion)

far left of each of the chart's four sections identifies the great geological eras into which the earth's history is divided by scientists, while the second column lists the archeological ages of human history. The key dates in the rise of life and of man's outstanding accomplishments appear in the third column (years and events mentioned in this volume of The Emergence of Man appear in bold type). The chart is not to scale; the reason is made clear by the bar below, which represents in linear scale the 4.5 billion years spanned by the chart—on the scaled bar, the portion relating to the total period of known human existence (far right) is too small to be distinguished.

Geology	Archeology	Years B.C.	
Holocene (cont.)	Neolithic New Stone Age	9000	
			Sheep domesticated in Near East
			Dog domesticated in North America
		8000	Jericho, oldest known city, settled
			Goat domesticated in Persia
			Man cultivates his first crops, wheat and barley, in Near East
		7000	Pattern of village life grows in Near East
			Catal Hüyük, in what is now Turkey, becomes largest Neolithic city
			Loom invented in Near East
			Cattle domesticated in Near East
		6000	Agriculture begins to replace hunting in Europe
			Copper used in trade in Mediterranean area
	Copper Age		Corn cultivated in Mexico
		4800	Oldest known massive stone monument built in Brittany
		4000	Sail-propelled boats used in Egypt
			First city-states develop in Sumer
			Cylinder seals begin to be used as marks of identification in Near East
		3500	First potatoes grown in South America
			Wheel originates in Sumer
			Man begins to cultivate rice in Far East
			Silk moth domesticated in China
			Horse domesticated in south Russia
			Egyptian merchant trading ships start to ply the Mediterranean
			Pictographic writing invented in Near East
	Bronze Age	3000	Bronze first used to make tools in Near East
			City life spreads to Nile Valley
			Plow is developed in Near East
			Accurate calendar based on stellar observation devised in Egypt
		2800	Stonehenge, most famous of ancient stone monuments, begun in England
			Pyramids built in Egypt
			Minoan navigators begin to venture into seas beyond the Mediterranean

Geology	Archeology	Years B.C.	
Holocene (cont.)	Bronze Age (cont.)	2600	Variety of gods and heroes glorified in Gilgamesh and other epics in Near East
		2500	Cities rise in the Indus Valley
			Earliest evidence of use of skis in Scandinavia
			Earliest written code of laws drawn up in Sumer
		2000	Use of bronze in Europe
			Chicken and elephant domesticated in Indus Valley
			Eskimo culture begins in Bering Strait area
		1500	Invention of ocean-going outrigger canoes enables man to reach islands of South Pacific
			Ceremonial bronze sculptures created in China
			Imperial government, ruling distant provinces, established by Hittites
		1400	Iron in use in Near East
			First complete alphabet devised in script of the Ugarit people in Syria
			Hebrews introduce concept of monotheism
	Iron Age	1000	Reindeer domesticated in Eurasia
			Phoenicians spread alphabet
		900	
		800	Use of iron begins to spread throughout Europe
			First highway system built in Assyria
			Homer composes Iliad and Odyssey
			Mounted nomads appear in the Near East as a new and powerful force
		700	Rome founded
			Wheel barrow invented in China
		200	Epics about India's gods and heroes, the Mahabharata and Ramayana, written
			Water wheel invented in Near East
		0	Christian era begins

▼ Two billion years ago ▼ One billion years ago

First oxygen-breathing animals (900 million) ▲   First animals to possess backbones (470 million) ▲   First men (1.3 million) ▲

Credits

The sources for the illustrations in this book are shown below. Credits from left to right are separated by semicolons, from top to bottom by dashes.

Cover—Painting by Michael A. Hampshire, background photograph by Roland and Sabrina Michaud from Rapho Guillumette. 8 —The Hermitage Museum, Leningrad/Werner Forman Archive. 11—Roger Viollet. 12, 13—Map by Rafael D. Palacios. 16, 17—Roland Michaud from Rapho Guillumette. 20, 21 —Herbert Maeder. 23—Novosti Press Agency courtesy Kiev State Historical Museum. 24—The Hermitage Museum, Leningrad/ Werner Forman Archive. 25—Novosti Press Agency courtesy Kiev State Historical Museum, except top right, The Hermitage Museum, Leningrad/Werner Forman Archive. 27 —Novosti Press Agency courtesy Kiev State Historical Museum. 29—Novosti Press Agency courtesy Archaeology Institute, Ukrainian Academy of Sciences, Kiev. 30, 31—Novosti Press Agency courtesy The Hermitage Museum, Leningrad. 32, 33—Novosti Press Agency courtesy Archaeology Institute, Ukrainian Academy of Sciences, Kiev. 34 —The Hermitage Museum, Leningrad/Werner Forman Archive; Dmitri Kessel, TIME-LIFE Picture Agency, © 1972 Time Incorporated courtesy The Hermitage Museum, Leningrad. 35—Sabine Weiss from Rapho Guillumette courtesy TIME-LIFE Picture Agency and The Hermitage Museum, Leningrad. 36, 37—The Hermitage Museum, Leningrad/Werner Forman Archive. 38, 39—Dmitri Kessel, TIME-LIFE Picture Agency, © 1972 Time Incorporated courtesy The Hermitage Museum, Leningrad. 40—Karel Neubert courtesy The Hermitage Museum, Leningrad, except bottom right, The Hermitage Museum, Leningrad/Werner Forman Archive. 44, 45 —Copyright © 1969 by C. J. Bucher Publishers Ltd., Switzerland, except bottom right, Dr. Jiri Volf. 46—Copyright © 1969 by C. J. Bucher Publishers Ltd., Switzerland—No credit. 48—Musée des Antiquités Nationales, Saint-Germain-en-Laye. 50, 51—Peter Kaplan. 54, 55—Painting by Don Bolognese; Sabine Weiss from Rapho Guillumette courtesy TIME-LIFE Picture Agency and The Hermitage Museum, Leningrad. 57—Dmitri Kessel, TIME-LIFE Picture Agency, © 1972 Time Incorporated courtesy The Hermitage Museum, Leningrad. 59—Maurice Chuzeville, Musée du Louvre, Paris, Collection David-Weill. 60, 61—Deutsches Archäologisches Institut, Athens—The British Museum, London. 62—Museo Civico Archeologico, Bologna—The British Museum, London. 63—The British Museum, London. 64, 65—C. M. Dixon courtesy The British Museum, London —Eileen Tweedy photograph from *The Royal Hordes* by E. D. Phillips © Thames & Hudson, 1965, London, courtesy The British Museum. 66—The Metropolitan Museum of Art, Rogers Fund, 1907—Courtesy of the Trustees of the British School of Archaeology at Athens. 67—The Hermitage Museum, Leningrad/Werner Forman Archive. 68—Karel Neubert courtesy The Hermitage Museum, Leningrad. 72—Drawings by Adolph E. Brotman. 73—Drawing by Adolph E. Brotman—Novosti Press Agency courtesy State Historical Museum, Moscow. 76, 77—Drawing by Don Bolognese. 78, 79—John Webb photograph from *The Royal Hordes* by E. D. Phillips © Thames & Hudson, 1965, London. 80, 81, 82, 83—The Metropolitan Museum of Art, Gift of the Dillon Fund, 1973. 85—*Stern/ Black Star.* 87—Novosti Press Agency courtesy The Hermitage Museum, Leningrad. 88 —C. M. Dixon courtesy The British Museum, London. 89—Dmitri Kessel, TIME-LIFE Picture Agency, © 1972 Time Incorporated courtesy The Hermitage Museum, Leningrad— The Hermitage Museum, Leningrad/Werner Forman Archive. 90—The Hermitage Museum, Leningrad/Werner Forman Archive. 91 —The British Museum, London—Dmitri Kessel, TIME-LIFE Picture Agency, © 1972 Time Incorporated courtesy The Hermitage Museum, Leningrad. 92—Karel Neubert courtesy The Hermitage Museum, Leningrad. 93—Novosti Press Agency courtesy The Hermitage Museum, Leningrad. 94—Novosti Press Agency courtesy The Hermitage Museum, Leningrad. 95—Novosti Press Agency courtesy The Hermitage Museum, Leningrad— Henry Groskinsky courtesy of Alice and Nasli Heeramaneck Collection, New York. 96, 97—Antikenabteilung, State Museum, Berlin. 98—The Hermitage Museum, Leningrad/Werner Forman Archive. 100—Culver Pictures. 102—Novosti Press Agency. 103 —Drawings by Adolph E. Brotman. 104— Novosti Press Agency. 105—Drawing by Adolph E. Brotman. 106—Novosti Press Agency courtesy The Hermitage Museum, Leningrad. 108—Novosti Press Agency courtesy The Hermitage Museum, Leningrad. 109 —Novosti Press Agency courtesy The Hermitage Museum, Leningrad except bottom right, C. M. Dixon courtesy The Hermitage Museum, Leningrad. 110—Novosti Press Agency courtesy The Hermitage Museum, Leningrad. 113—C. M. Dixon courtesy The Hermitage Museum, Leningrad; From *Frozen Tombs of the Scythians* by M. I. Artamonov. Copyright © May 1965 by Scientic American, Inc. All rights reserved. 114—Editions Cercle d'Art, Paris. 117 through 125—Paintings by Michael A. Hampshire. 126—Mehmet Ali Kislali courtesy Topkapi Sarayi Museum, Istanbul. 128—Courtesy of L. Carrington Goodrich. 131, 132, 133—Editions Cercle d'Art, Paris. 134—Sabine Weiss from Rapho Guillumette courtesy TIME-LIFE Picture Agency and The Hermitage Museum, Leningrad; Dmitri Kessel, TIME-LIFE Picture Agency, © 1972 Time Incorporated courtesy The Hermitage Museum, Leningrad. 136 through 140—Mehmet Ali Kislali courtesy Topkapi Sarayi Museum, Istanbul. 143 through 153—Museum für Völkerkunde, Hamburg.

Acknowledgments

For the help given in the preparation of this book, the editors are particularly indebted to the American School of Classical Studies, Athens, Greece; Pierre Amiet, Chief Curator, and Françoise Tallon, Researcher, Department of Oriental Antiquities, Louvre Museum, Paris; Thomas Barfield, Department of Anthropology, Harvard University, Cambridge, Massachusetts; British School of Classical Studies, Athens, Greece; Henri Delporte, Curator, Christiane Eluère, Museum of National Antiquities, Saint-Germain-en-Laye, France; Department of Western Asiatic Antiquities, British Museum, London; Ann R. Farkas, New York City; Marilyn Fu, Assistant Curator, Department of Far Eastern Art, Metropolitan Museum of Art, New York City; German Institute of Archaeology, Athens, Greece; L. Carrington Goodrich, Professor Emeritus of Chinese, Columbia University, New York City; Dr. Franz Hampl, National Museum of Lower Austria, Vienna; John F. Haskins, Professor of Oriental Art History, University of Pittsburgh, Pennsylvania; Heinz Heck, Director, Roland Lindemann, Catskill Game Farm, Catskill, New York; Galina Ignatieva, Researcher, Novosti Press Agency, Moscow; Karl Jettmar, Professor, South Asian Institute, University of Heidelberg, Germany; Vera Kovarsky, Purdy Station, New York; Thomas Lawton, Assistant Director, Freer Gallery of Art, Smithsonian Institution, Washington, D.C.; Guglielmo Maetzke, Superintendency for Etruscan Antiquities, Florence, Italy; Herbert Melichar, Professor, Department of Prehistory, Museum of Natural History, Vienna, Austria; Karen Rubinson, New York City; Richard H. Tedford, Curator, Department of Vertebrate Paleontology, American Museum of Natural History, New York City; Maurizio Tosi, Italian Institute for Middle and Far Eastern Studies, Rome; Brian Spooner, Assistant Curator of Near Eastern Ethnography, University Museum, Philadelphia, Pennsylvania; Rüdiger Vossen, Ethnological Museum, Hamburg, Germany. Quotes on page 52 from *Ancient Greek Horsemanship* by J. K. Anderson, originally published by the University of California Press; reprinted by permission of The Regents of the University of California. Quotations from Herodotus based on a translation by George Rawlinson. Everyman's Library, J. M. Dent & Sons Ltd., 1910.

Bibliography

Anderson, J. K., *Ancient Greek Horseman-ship*. University of California Press, 1961.

Artamonov, M. I., *The Splendor of Scythian Art*. Frederick A. Praeger, 1969.

Atkinson, Thomas Witlam, *Oriental and Western Siberia*. Praeger Publishers, 1970.

Bacon, Elizabeth E., *Central Asians under Russian Rule*. Cornell University Press, 1966.

Borovka, Gregory, *Scythian Art*. Paragon Book Reprint Company, 1967.

Bunker, Emma C., C. Bruce Chatwin, and Ann R. Farkas, *Animal Style Art from East to West*. Asia House Gallery, 1970.

Burney, Charles, and David Marshall Lang, *The Peoples of the Hills*. Weidenfeld and Nicolson, 1971.

Cardona, George, Henry M. Hoenigswald, and Alfred Senn, *Indo-European and Indo-Europeans*. University of Pennsylvania Press, 1970.

Carter, Dagny, *The Symbol of the Beast*. The Ronald Press Company, 1957.

Charrière, Georges, *L'Art Barbare Scythe*. Editions Cercle d'Art, 1971.

Chenevix-Trench, Charles, *A History of Horsemanship*. Doubleday & Company, Inc., 1970.

Dalton, O. M., *The Treasure of the Oxus*. The Trustees of the British Museum, 1964.

Epstein, H., *Domestic Animals of China*. Africana Publishing Corporation, 1971.

Forde, Daryll C., *Habitat, Economy and Society*. E. P. Dutton, 1935.

Gimbutas, Marija, *Bronze Age Cultures in Central and Eastern Europe*. Mouton & Co., 1965.

Godolphin, Francis R. B., *The Greek Histo-rians*, Vol. I. Random House, 1942.

Grant, Michael, *The Ancient Historians*. Charles Scribner's Sons, 1970.

Howey, M. Oldfield, *The Horse in Magic and Myth*. William Rider & Son, Ltd., 1923.

Ipsiroglu, M. S., *Painting and Culture of the Mongols*. Harry N. Abrams, Inc., no date.

Isenbart, H. H., and E. M. Buhrer, *The King-dom of the Horse*. C. J. Bucher, Ltd., 1969.

Jettmar, Karl, *Art of the Steppes*. Crown Publishers, 1964.

Latham, Ronald, trans., *The Travels of Mar-co Polo*. Penguin Books, 1958.

Lattimore, Owen:
Inner Asian Frontiers of China. Beacon Press, 1962.
Studies in Frontier History. Oxford University Press, 1962.

Leskov, A., *Treasures from the Ukrainian Barrows*. Aurora Art Publishers, no date.

Levin, M. G., and L. P. Potapov, eds., *The Peoples of Siberia*. University of Chicago Press, 1964.

McGovern, William Montgomery, *The Early Empires of Central Asia*. University of North Carolina Press, 1939.

Masson, V. M., and V. I. Sarianidi, *Central Asia*. Thames and Hudson, 1972.

Michael, Henry N., ed., *Studies in Siberian Shamanism*. Anthropology of the North, No. 4. University of Toronto Press, 1963.

Minns, Ellis H., *Scythians and Greeks*. Biblo and Tannen, 1971.

Mohr, Erna, *The Asiatic Wild Horse*. Translated from the German by Daphne Machin Goodall. J. A. Allen & Co., Inc., 1971.

Mongait, A. L., *Archaeology in the U.S.S.R.* Penguin Books, 1961.

Needham, Joseph, et al., *Science and Civilization in China*. Vol. IV, Part 3. Cam-bridge University Press, 1971.

Parker, W. H., *The Soviet Union*. Aldine Publishing Company, 1969.

Phillips, E. D.:
The Mongols. Frederick A. Praeger, 1969.
The Royal Hordes. McGraw-Hill Book Company, 1965.

Piggott, Stuart, ed., *The Dawn of Civiliza-tion*. McGraw-Hill Book Company, 1967.

Rice, Tamara Talbot, *The Scythians*. Frederick A. Praeger, 1957.

Rudenko, S. I., *Frozen Tombs of Siberia*. University of California Press, 1970.

Simpson, George Gaylord, *Horses*. Oxford University Press, 1951.

Singer, Charles, E. J. Holmyard, and A. R. Hall, eds., *A History of Technology*, Vol. I. Oxford University Press, 1954.

Strommenger, Eva, *5000 Years of the Art of Mesopotamia*. Harry N. Abrams, Inc., no date.

Sulimirski, Tadeusz:
Prehistoric Russia. Humanities Press, 1970.
The Sarmatians. Praeger Publishers, 1970.

Tannahill, Reay, *Food in History*. Stein and Day, 1973.

Tolstov, Sergei Pavlovich, *Peoples of the World*. Ethnographic Studies, Vol. II. Academy of Sciences, Institute of Ethnography, 1963. (In Russian.)

Ucko, Peter J., and G. W. Dimbleby, eds., *The Domestication and Exploitation of Plants and Animals*. Aldine Publishing Company, 1969.

Yadin, Yigael, *The Art of Warfare in Bib-lical Lands*. Weidenfeld and Nicolson, 1963.

Zeuner, Frederick E., *A History of Domes-ticated Animals*. Harper & Row, 1963.

Index

Printed in U.S.A. **X**

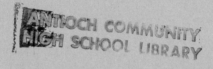